THE 5 *Apology* LANGUAGES

THE 5 Apology LANGUAGES

The Secret to Healthy Relationships

Gary Chapman
Jennifer Thomas

NORTHFIELD PUBLISHING

CHICAGO

Edited by Elizabeth Cody Newenhuyse
Interior design: Puckett Smartt
Cover design: Erik M. Peterson
Cover image: Light bokeh courtesy of Scott Hewitt, Unsplash
Author photo of Gary Chapman: Grooters Productions
Author photo of Jennifer Thomas: Ross Thomas Photography

Library of Congress Cataloging-in-Publication Data

Names: Chapman, Gary D., 1938- author. | Thomas, Jennifer, 1969- author.
Title: The 5 apology languages : the secret to healthy relationships / Gary
    Chapman, Jennifer Thomas.
Other titles: Five languages of apology | Five apology languages
Description: Chicago : Northfield Publishing, [2022] | Revised and updated
    edition of When Sorry Isn't Enough, originally published in 2006 as: The
    five languages of apology : how to experience healing in all your
    relationships. | Includes bibliographical references. | Summary:
    "Whether fractured by major incident or minor irritation, the emotions
    provoked can often feel insurmountable, preventing a relationship from
    moving forward and the offended from moving on. Discover why certain
    apologies clear the path for emotional healing, reconciliation, and
    freedom, while others fall desperately short"-- Provided by publisher.
Identifiers: LCCN 2021043381 (print) | LCCN 2021043382 (ebook) | ISBN
    9780802428691 (paperback) | ISBN 9780802475039 (ebook)
Subjects: LCSH: Apologizing. | Remorse. | Forgiveness--Religious
    aspects--Christianity. | Interpersonal relations--Religious
    aspects--Christianity. | BISAC: FAMILY & RELATIONSHIPS / Conflict
    Resolution | RELIGION / Christian Living / Family & Relationships
Classification: LCC BF575.A75 C43 2022 (print) | LCC BF575.A75 (ebook) |
    DDC 158.2--dc23
LC record available at https://lccn.loc.gov/2021043381
LC ebook record available at https://lccn.loc.gov/2021043382

We hope you enjoy this book from Northfield Publishing. Our goal is to provide high-quality, thought-provoking books and products that connect truth to your real needs and challenges. For more information on other books and products that will help you with all your important relationships, go to northfieldpublishing.com or write to:

Northfield Publishing
820 N. LaSalle Boulevard
Chicago, IL 60610

5 7 9 10 8 6 4

Printed in the United States of America

To Karolyn, who has accepted my apologies
and extended forgiveness
many times through our five decades
as husband and wife

———

To my children—Ross, Lydia, and Russell.
My love for you knows no bounds.

Contents

INTRODUCTION

Why This Is Important

"My daughter is late over and over again," a woman said to me. "She's a wonderful young woman, but she's just habitually late—to our house for dinner, to church, you name it. It isn't a huge deal, but I wish just once she would say she was sorry."

Another woman I'll call Lisa said, "I love my husband dearly, but I'm tired of repeated apologies without behavior change, especially when it comes to chores. Don't just say, 'I'm sorry I forgot to mop the kitchen floor.' Remember to do it!"

Jack, fiftyish, is estranged from his brother because years ago his brother swindled him out of some money. "Never has he told me he feels bad about what he did. I don't really care about the money, but I feel like he should make it right somehow," he said.

Michelle is recently divorced from Sam. However, she recognizes her part in the disintegration of their marriage, and God is leading her to seek reconciliation: "Deep down, I believe that God is saying it is worth it to pursue this often untraveled road." These offenses range from annoying to life-shattering—but in every case, a relationship needs mending. A wrong needs to be righted. Where do we start?

Sara was wondering the same thing when she came to one of my marriage seminars. Before the conference started, she came up to me and asked, "Are you going to deal with the importance of apologizing?"

"That's an interesting topic," I responded. "Why do you ask?"

"Well, all my husband says is 'I'm sorry.' To me, that's not an apology."

"So what do you want him to say or do?" I asked.

"I want him to admit that he is wrong and to ask me to forgive him. I also want him to assure me that it won't happen again."

Dr. Jennifer Thomas and I have conducted extensive research on the importance of apologizing effectively, and what we have learned has convinced us that Sara is not alone in her desire to deal with issues of admitting wrong and seeking forgiveness. *Apology*, however, is not a word that means the same thing to everyone. That is because we have different "languages" of apology.

"I have seen this often in my counseling," Jennifer said. "One spouse says, 'If he would only apologize,' and the other says, 'I have apologized.' So they get into an argument about what it means to apologize. Of course, they have different perceptions."

I have observed numerous couples in my office exhibiting similar behavior. It was obvious they were not connecting with each other. The supposed apology was not having the desired effect of forgiveness and reconciliation. I also remember occasions in my own marriage when Karolyn would apologize but I considered it rather weak, and other occasions when I would apologize, but she'd have a hard time forgiving me because she felt that I was insincere.

We believe that going beyond a quick "I'm sorry"—learning to apologize effectively—can help rekindle love that has been dimmed by pain. We believe that when we all learn to apologize—and when we understand each other's apology language—we can trade in tired excuses for honesty, trust, and joy.

All of us are painfully aware of the conflict, division, anger, and strife in our world today. We will conclude, therefore, with a chapter that some may see as ethereal but we believe holds great potential: What would the world be like if we all learned to apologize effectively?

Join us as we explore what it means to be truly sorry—and to move toward true forgiveness.

—Gary Chapman, PhD
—Jennifer Thomas, PhD

THE 5 Apology LANGUAGES

Righting Wrongs

In a perfect world, there would be no need for apologies. However, because the world is imperfect, we cannot survive without them. My academic background is the field of anthropology, the study of human culture. One of the clear conclusions of the anthropologist is that all people have a sense of morality: Some things are right, and some things are wrong. People are incurably moral. In psychology, it is often called the conscience. In theology, it may be referred to as the "sense of *ought*" or the imprint of the divine.

It is true that the standard by which the conscience condemns or affirms is influenced by the culture. For example, in Eskimo (or Inuit) culture, if one is on a trek and runs out of food, it is perfectly permissible to enter the igloo of a stranger and eat whatever is available. In most other Western cultures, to enter an unoccupied house would be considered "breaking and entering," an offense punishable as a crime. Although the standard of right will differ from culture to culture and sometimes within cultures, all people have a sense of right and wrong.

When one's sense of right is violated, that person will experience anger. He or she will feel wronged and resentful at the person who has violated their trust. The wrongful act stands as a barrier between the two people, and the relationship is fractured. They cannot, even if they desired, live as though the wrong had not been committed. Jack, whose brother swindled him years ago, says, "Things have never been the same between us." Whatever the offense, something inside the offended calls for justice. It is these human realities that serve as the basis of all judicial systems.

A CRY FOR RECONCILIATION

While justice may bring some sense of satisfaction to the offended person, justice does not typically restore relationships. If an employee who is found stealing from the company is caught, tried, and fined or imprisoned, everyone says, "Justice has been served." But the company is not likely to restore the employee to the original place of leadership. On the other hand, if an employee steals from the company but quickly takes responsibility for the error, reports that misdeed to the supervisor, expresses sincere regret, offers to pay for all inequities, and pleads for mercy, there is the possibility that the employee will be allowed to continue with the company.

Humankind has an amazing capacity to forgive. I remember a number of years ago visiting the town of Coventry, England. I stood in the shell of a cathedral that had been bombed by the Nazis in the Second World War. I listened as the guide told the story of the new cathedral that rose beside the ruins. Some years after the war, a group of Germans had come and helped build the new cathedral as an act of contrition for the damages their fellow countrymen had inflicted. Everyone had agreed to allow the ruins to remain in the shadow of the new cathedral. Both structures were symbolic: the one of man's inhumanity to man, the other of the power of forgiveness and reconciliation.

Something within us cries out for reconciliation when wrongdoing has fractured a relationship. The desire for reconciliation is often more potent than the desire for justice. The more intimate the relationship, the deeper the desire for reconciliation. When a husband treats his wife unfairly, in her hurt and anger she is pulled between a longing for justice and a desire for mercy. On the one hand, she wants him to pay for his wrongdoing; on the other hand, she wishes for reconciliation. It is his sincere apology that makes genuine reconciliation possible. If there is no apology, then her sense of morality pushes her to demand justice. Many times through the years, I have observed divorce proceedings and watched the judge seek to determine what was just. I have often wondered if sincere apologies would have changed the sad outcome.

I have looked into the eyes of teenage rage and wondered how different life would be if an abusive father had apologized. Without apologies, anger builds and pushes us to demand justice. When, as we see it, justice is not forthcoming, we often take matters into our own hands and seek revenge on those who have wronged us. Anger escalates and can end in violence. The man who walks into the office of his former employer and shoots his supervisor and three of his coworkers burns with a sense of injustice—to the point where only murderous revenge will right the wrong. Things might have been different had he had the courage to lovingly confront—and others had the courage to say, "I was wrong."

CAN YOU FORGIVE WITHOUT AN APOLOGY?

Genuine forgiveness and reconciliation are two-person transactions that are enabled by apologies. Some, particularly within the Christian worldview, have taught forgiveness without an apology. They often quote the words of Jesus, "If you do not forgive men their trespasses, neither will your Father forgive your trespasses."[1] Thus, they say to the wife whose husband has been unfaithful and continues in his adulterous affair, "You must forgive him, or God will not forgive you." Such an interpretation of Jesus' teachings fails to reckon with the rest of the scriptural teachings on forgiveness. The Christian is instructed to forgive others in the same manner that God forgives us. How does God forgive us? The Scriptures say that if we confess our sins, God will forgive our sins.[2] Nothing in the Old or New Testaments indicates that God forgives the sins of people who do not confess and repent of their sins.

When a pastor encourages a wife to forgive her erring husband while he still continues in his wrongdoing, the minister is requiring of the wife something that God Himself does not do. Jesus' teaching is that we are to be always willing to forgive, as God is always willing to forgive those who repent. Some will object to this idea, indicating that Jesus forgave those who were killing Him, but that is not what the Scriptures say. Rather, Jesus prayed, "Father, forgive them, for they do not know what they are doing."[3] Jesus expressed His heartfelt compassion and His desire to see His murderers forgiven. That should be our desire and our prayer. Their forgiveness came later when they acknowledged that they had indeed killed the Son of God.[4]

Forgiveness without an apology is often encouraged for the benefit of the forgiver rather than the benefit of the offender. Such forgiveness does not lead to reconciliation. When there is no apology, the

Christian is encouraged to release the person to God for justice[5] and to release one's anger to God through forbearance.[6]

Dietrich Bonhoeffer, the great theologian who was martyred by the Nazis in a concentration camp in 1945, argued against the "preaching of forgiveness without requiring repentance." He referred to such forgiveness as "cheap grace . . . which amounts to the justification of sin without the justification of the repentant sinner."[7]

Genuine forgiveness removes the barrier that was created by the offense and opens the door to restoring trust over time. If the relationship was warm and intimate before the offense, it can become loving again. If the relationship was simply one of casual acquaintance, it may grow to a deeper level through the dynamic process of forgiveness. If the offense was created by an unknown person such as a rapist or a murderer, there was no relationship to be restored. If they have apologized and you have forgiven, each of you is free to go on living your lives, although the criminal will still face the judicial system created by the culture to deal with deviant behavior.

THE FIVE-GALLON CONTAINER

When we apologize, we accept responsibility for our behavior, seeking to make amends with the person who was offended. Genuine apology opens the door to the possibility of forgiveness and reconciliation. Then we can continue to build the relationship. Without apology, the offense sits as a barrier, and the quality of the relationship is diminished. Good relationships are always marked by a willingness to apologize, forgive, and reconcile.

Sincere apologies also assuage a guilty conscience. Picture your conscience as a five-gallon container strapped to your back. Whenever you wrong another, it's like pouring a gallon of liquid into your conscience. Three or four wrongs and your conscience is getting full—and you are getting heavy. A full conscience leaves one with a sense of guilt and shame. The only way to effectively empty the conscience is to apologize to God and the person you offended. When this is done, you can look God in the face, you can look yourself in the mirror, and you can look the other person in the eye, not because you are perfect but because you have been willing to take responsibility for your failure.

We may or may not have learned the art of apologizing when we were children. In healthy families, parents teach their children to apologize. However, many children grow up in dysfunctional families where hurt, anger, and bitterness are a way of life, and no one ever apologizes.

WHAT REAL LOVE LOOKS LIKE

The good news is that the art of apology can be learned. What we have discovered in our research is that there are five fundamental aspects of an apology. We call them the five languages of apology. Each of them is important, but for some people, one or two of the languages may communicate more effectively than the others. The key to good relationships is learning the apology language of the other person and being willing to speak it. When you speak their primary language, you make it easier for them to hear your sincerity and to genuinely forgive you.

Understanding and applying the five languages of an apology will greatly enhance all your relationships.

In the next five chapters, we will explain the five languages. In chapter 7, we will show you how to discover both your own and another person's primary apology language and how this can make your efforts at apologizing most productive.

Love often means saying you're sorry—over and over again. Real love will be marked by apologies by the offender and forgiveness by the offended. This is the path to restored, loving relationships. It all begins by learning to speak the right language of apology when you offend someone.

TALK ABOUT IT

Here are a number of questions designed to spark interaction and stimulate thought. Share these with your spouse or close friend or in a small group, or use them for personal reflection.

Discuss the author's observation, "People are incurably moral." Agree? Disagree?

Share a story you've heard or experience you've had showing humankind's "amazing capacity to forgive."

Those we care about most are those most affected by our apologies. Who are the people in your life who will be most affected by your learning in the area of apology?

EXPRESSING
REGRET

"I'm Sorry"

EXPRESSING REGRET

It starts really early. Little Ava or little Oliver pushes another child at preschool. The kid cries. The teacher comforts them and then turns to the small perpetrator. "Tell William you're sorry." Ava or Oliver looks down and mumbles, "I'm sorry." The kids go back to their play. Crisis averted.

But is it enough?

Maybe not always, as we shall see. But it does form the basis of our first language of apology: *expressing regret*. Expressing regret is the emotional aspect of an apology. It is expressing to the offended person your own sense of guilt, shame, and pain that your behavior has hurt him deeply. It is interesting that when Robert Fulghum wrote his book *All I Really Need to Know I Learned in Kindergarten*, he included as one of the things he learned: "Say you're sorry when you hurt some-body."[1] Expressing regret is fundamental to good relationships.

Apology is birthed in the womb of regret. We regret the pain we have caused, the disappointment, the inconvenience, the betrayal of trust. Regret focuses on what you did or failed to do and how it affected the other person. The offended one is experiencing painful emotions, and they want you to feel some of their pain. They want some evidence that you realize how deeply you have hurt them. For some people, this is the one thing they listen for in an apology. Without the expression of regret, they do not sense that the apology is adequate or sincere.

SAYING THE MAGIC WORDS

A simple "I'm sorry" can go a long way toward restoring goodwill. The absence of the words "I'm sorry" stands out to some like a very sore thumb. Quite often offenders will not realize that they have left out some "magic words," but you can be assured that the listener is scanning the silence for those missing words.

Let me (Jennifer) share a personal story. Last spring, I was part of a group of women who received end-of-the-year prizes for each having led a small group. I selected my prize from a sales consultant's catalog and was eagerly awaiting the arrival of my thank-you gift. The summer came and went with no delivery of my product. I began to wonder, *Where is my order?* When the end of the year came with no package, I concluded that my order was not likely to come. I actually decided at that time that it was not worth pursuing the issue with anyone. I reasoned that I had enjoyed leading the group and put the item out of my mind with the refrain, "Easy come, easy go."

Imagine my surprise when I received a telephone message from the consultant the next spring. She said that she had been cleaning out boxes and found my order! She closed the phone message by saying simply that she wanted to arrange to get the item to me. For my part, I was pleasantly surprised to be in the position to receive that which I had let go. However, something was nagging at me. I replayed her message and confirmed my suspicion: She had failed to say, "I am sorry for my mistake," or to express any sort of regret. I would have quickly embraced such an apology.

As it was, I pondered the issue in my mind long enough to write it down and to wonder how often I might do the same thing. Do I correct problems, yet not assume responsibility or express regret? The magic words "I'm sorry" would have made a world of difference to me.

"I WANT HIM TO UNDERSTAND HOW HE HURT ME"

Many people can identify with Jennifer's experience. Melissa has been married to her husband, Pete, for twenty-seven years. When I asked her, "What do you look for in an apology when Pete has wronged you?" her immediate response was, "Most of all I want him to understand how he hurt me and why. I want him to see things from my perspective. I expect to hear him say, 'I apologize. I am really sorry.'

"It helps if he gives an explanation of how his actions have hurt me. That way, I know he understands. If it's something really bad, I expect abject misery and want him to really be sad about the pain he caused me."

I asked, "When you say 'really bad,' what kind of things do you have in mind?"

"Like the time he took a woman at the office out to lunch without telling me. I heard it from a friend, and I was really hurt. I think if he had tried to justify it, I would have never gotten over it. You see, my husband is not the kind of man who takes other women out to lunch. I knew he had to have a little fascination for her or he would not have done it. He admitted that I was right and told me how sorry he was.

He said that he knew that I would never go out with another man and that if I did, he would be deeply hurt. He said that he regretted what he had done and wished he had never done it. I knew he was sincere when I saw tears come to his eyes." For Melissa, the heart of an apology is a sincere expression of regret.

WHAT DOES YOUR BODY SAY?

It is important that our body language agree with the words we are saying if we expect the offended person to sense our sincerity. Melissa mentioned Pete's tears as evidence of his sincerity. Listen to the words of another wife who said, "I know when my husband sincerely feels sorry for something he's done, because he becomes very quiet and his physical mannerisms become introverted. He apologizes with a soft voice and a bowed head. This shows me that he feels really bad. Then I know it's genuine."

Robert and Katie have been married for seven years. When I asked him, "How do you know that Katie is sincere when she apologizes?" his answer was, "Eye contact. If she looks me in the eye and says 'I'm sorry,' I know she's sincere. If she says 'I'm sorry' while passing through the room, I know she's hiding something. A hug and a kiss after the apology also let me know that she's sincere."

Robert is illustrating the reality that sometimes our body language speaks louder than our spoken language. This is especially true when the two contradict each other. For example, one wife said, "When he screams at me, 'I said I'm sorry!' but his eyes are glaring and his hands are shaking, it's like he's trying to make me forgive him. It seems to me he is more concerned about moving on and forgetting it than truly apologizing. It's like my hurt doesn't matter—let's just get on with life."

SORRY FOR WHAT?

An apology has more impact when it's specific. LuAnn captured this idea when she said, "I expect the apologizer to say 'I'm sorry for____' and then be specific about what they are sorry about." When we're specific, we communicate to the offended person that we truly understand how much we have hurt him or her. Specificity places the focus on our action and how it affected the other person.

The more details we can give, the better. If I (Jennifer) stood someone up for a movie, I wouldn't just say, "I'm sorry I didn't make it to the movie." It would mean more to the person if I could list all the ways my action affected her. "I know that you left your home on time; you stopped what you were doing. You made it down here during rush-hour traffic; you had to wait and be concerned about my well-being. I know that you like to see the entire picture, and for you, my neglect may have made you unable to enjoy the movie since you missed the beginning. I can imagine how upset I would have been if a friend had done this to me. You have a right to be angry, disappointed, frustrated, and hurt—and I want you to know that I am sincerely sorry for my irresponsibility."

The details reveal the depth of your understanding of the situation and how much you inconvenienced your friend.

"WHAT KIND OF AN APOLOGY IS THAT?"

Sincere regret also needs to stand alone. It should not be followed with "But . . ." Rodney, who has been married three years to his second wife, Simone, says, "I know that my wife means it when she says, 'I'm sorry. I know that I hurt you by yelling at you.' Then she does not go on to accuse me of causing her to get upset. My first wife always blamed me for everything."

Numerous individuals in our research made statements similar to this. "She apologizes, but then turns it around and blames her actions on something *I* did."

Brenda remembers well one of her husband's failed attempts at apologizing—it happened the night before they would attend one of my marriage seminars. Her husband went to a coworker's fiftieth birthday party, leaving Brenda at home with their four children. Because her husband normally worked a 10 p.m. to 6 a.m. shift, she had hoped for valuable evening time together.

"Even though I was angry, he left and said that he would be back in an hour," Brenda recalls. "Two hours later when we were all in bed, he shows up. He apologized but added that I was acting like a baby, and he has a right to go out.

"So whatever words he was saying to apologize weren't helping, since he was putting me down. I also prayed that when he got home, I wouldn't have a bad attitude. But I was so filled with anger that it didn't work."

Anytime we verbally shift the blame to the other person, we have moved from an apology to an attack. Attacks never lead to forgiveness and reconciliation.

Megan is a twenty-nine-year-old single who has been in a committed dating relationship for three years. She said, "Anytime an apology is followed by an excuse for the offense, the excuse cancels out the apology in my mind. Just own up that, intentionally or not, you hurt me or didn't meet my expectations. Don't apologize and then make excuses for your offense. Leave it at the apology."

As sisters, Juanita and Jasmine were often in conflict. They each wanted to have a better relationship, but neither seemed to know how. When I asked Jasmine, "Does Juanita ever apologize when she loses her temper?" Jasmine said, "Oh, all the time, but then she'll say something like, 'I just wish you would stop putting me down. I know I'm not as educated as you, but that doesn't mean that you can treat me like dirt.' What kind of an apology is that? She puts all the blame on me."

APOLOGIES THAT DO NOT MANIPULATE

An expression of sincere regret should not manipulate the other person into reciprocating. Natalie and George have been dating for two years and are going through some rough waters. She said, "George has at times said he was sorry. But then he expects me to say it back, even if I don't feel like I should have to because *he* was the cause of the fight in the first place. That just doesn't work for me. I want him to say he's sorry and not expect anything in return. That would mean that he is truly sorry."

Sometimes we hurt people and don't realize it. It was certainly not intentional. Good relationships are fostered by expressing regret even when we did not intend to hurt them. If I bump into someone getting out of an elevator, I murmur, "I'm sorry," not because I intentionally bumped him but because I identify with his inconvenience or irritation with my unintentional bump. The same principle is true in close relationships. You may not realize that your behavior has upset your spouse, but when it becomes apparent, then you can say, "I'm sorry that my behavior caused you so much pain. I didn't intend to hurt you."

Regret focuses on dealing with one's own behavior and expressing empathy for the hurt it has caused the other person. Insincerity is also communicated when we say "I'm sorry" simply to get the other person to stop confronting us with the issue. Rhonda sensed this when she said, "Early in our marriage, my husband did something really damaging. He absolutely refused to be sorry or change. Then eventually he said that he was sorry, but it was only to get me off his back. His actions spoke more loudly than his words, indicating 'Drop it! I want to get out of this trap.' He didn't see that what he had done was wrong and how much he had hurt me."

"I HOPE YOU CAN FORGIVE ME"

Writing a letter of apology may help to underscore your sincerity. To put your apology in writing may give it more emotional weight, because your spouse or friend can read it again and again. The process of writing may also help you clarify your regrets and verbalize them in a positive way. Here is a letter that one of my (Jennifer's) clients received from her husband. She has given me permission to share it.

Dear Olivia,

I want to apologize for being late tonight and for not letting you know as soon as I could anticipate that I would be late again. I know this was an awfully difficult day for you with the kids. I wish so much I could have been here to help, or at least been on time to relieve you. My heart broke when at 6:30 p.m. I got your message from 4:45 p.m. with your cry for help and request that I be home on time. I hated to think that every moment from then on you must have been listening for my return. I really regret that my not setting good boundaries with my boss forced you to carry an extra burden today. I will strive to be more reliable. I am sorry, and I hope you can forgive me.

With contrition, your loving husband,

Jon

Olivia wrote at the bottom of the page, "Forgiven," and the date. Obviously, Jon's expression of regret got through to Olivia. She sensed his sincerity and was willing to forgive him.

THE POWER OF "I'M SORRY"

Look at what the following people had to say about apology language #1: *expressing regret.*

"My husband had made comments in front of our friends about my being overweight and eating too much. I was so hurt. Later that night, he said that he knew the situation was very uncomfortable for me and he was sorry for what he had done to create the situation by his hurtful words. I forgave him because I felt he was sincere."

—Paula, age fifty-three, married eleven years to her second husband

"I want an apology that comes from the heart, that is truly sorry for the action that caused my hurt. In other words, I want them to feel bad for making me feel bad."

—Lily, age twenty-six and single

"He came home late one night, but he apologized for disappointing me. I told him it was okay; I understood. He continued by saying that he still did not like to disappoint me; that made me feel really good."

—Marina, age twenty-eight, married two years

"[It's a genuine apology] when she expresses true feelings of regret, expresses understanding of my feelings, and acts like she is sorry that she hurt me."

—Charles, age forty, married for ten years

"I want to see that they feel guilty for what they did or said and are truly sorry."

—Todd, age thirty-four and single

For these and many others, the language of expressing regret is extremely important in the process of healing and restoration. If you want these people to sense your sincerity, then you must learn to speak the language of regret, which focuses on their pain and your behavior and how the two are related. It is communicating to them that you feel hurt because you know your actions have hurt them. It is this identification with their pain that stimulates in them a willingness to forgive.

If you are willing to express regret, here are some statements that may help you do so.

STATEMENTS OF REGRET

I know now that I hurt you very deeply. That causes me immense pain. I am truly sorry for what I did.

I feel really bad that I disappointed you. I should have been more thoughtful. I'm sorry that I caused you so much pain.

At the time, obviously I was not thinking very well. I never intended to hurt you, but now I can see that my words were way out of line. I'm sorry that I was so insensitive.

I am sorry that I violated your trust. I've created a roadblock in our relationship that I want to remove. I understand that even after I apologize, it may take awhile for you to venture down the road of trust with me again.

You were promised a service that we have not provided. I am sorry that our company clearly dropped the ball this time.

TALK ABOUT IT

Have you had childhood experiences similar to those described at the beginning of this chapter? Is there anyone from your past that you would like to say "I'm sorry" to?

Have you ever hurt someone without realizing it? What did you do when you became aware that you had hurt someone? What would most people say they are looking for in an apology?

ACCEPTING
RESPONSIBILITY

3

"I Was Wrong"

ACCEPTING RESPONSIBILITY

As a boss, Larry usually stayed calm, but on this particular day he ran out of patience. He spoke harshly to one of his employees. The message was true and the reproof needed, but he had spoken in anger and his words had been cutting. Afterward, he felt bad but told himself, *What I said was true, and the guy needs to shape up. He needs to know I'm not a pushover.*

Jane had trouble remembering appointments, especially those that fell on the weekend when she often failed to look at her calendar. Now she was again arriving halfway through a neighborhood planning meeting. Jane's mind ran through lists of reasons for her confusion about the meeting time. At the top of the list was her recent return from a cross-country trip. She didn't know what day it was, much less what time it was. Meanwhile, the others at the meeting felt she owed them an apology for again showing up late.

Young Shawn was in pain following a medical procedure. His

mom was hovering, trying to make him comfortable and insisting that he take his pain medication. Unfortunately, Shawn swatted away his well-meaning mother. Shawn knew that his action was unkind and degrading, but he told himself, *Medicine can make anyone act crazy. My mom should understand.*

Three different scenarios: unkind words, failure to come through, and lashing out. Larry, Jane, and Shawn all felt a tug of guilt. However, their excuses, they felt, covered their need to apologize.

Such actions have fractured relationships. A simple apology could make a world of difference—but an apology means accepting responsibility for one's actions.

Why is it so difficult for some of us to say "I was wrong"? Often our reluctance to admit wrongdoing is tied to our sense of self-worth. To admit that we are wrong is perceived as weakness. We may reason, *Only losers confess. Intelligent people try to show that their actions were justified.*

The seeds of this self-justifying tendency are often planted in childhood. When a child is excessively punished, condemned, or shamed for minor offenses, the sense of self-worth is diminished. Subconsciously, the child makes the emotional link between wrong behavior and low self-worth. Thus, to admit wrong is to be "bad." The child who grows up with this emotional pattern will have difficulty admitting wrongdoing as an adult because to do so strikes at his or her self-esteem.

The good news is that as adults, we can understand these negative emotional patterns and yet not be imprisoned by them. The reality is there are no perfect adults. Mature adults learn how to break the harmful patterns of childhood and accept responsibility for their own failures, but immature adults are forever rationalizing their own bad behavior.

"IT'S NOT MY FAULT"

Such rationalization often takes the form of blaming others. We may admit that what we did or said was not the best, but our behavior was provoked by the other person's irresponsible actions. Thus, we blame others and find it difficult to admit, "I was wrong." Such blaming is also a sign of immaturity. Children by nature blame others for their negative behavior. I remember a time when my six-year-old son, confronted with knocking a glass off the table that now lay shattered on the floor, explained, "It did it by itself." To this day, my wife and I will jokingly say to each other when confronted with an irresponsible action, "It did it by itself." We both know that we are joking, but it feels so good to place the blame on "it" rather than "me."

Mature adults learn to accept responsibility for their behavior, whereas immature adults continue with childish fantasies and tend to blame others for their mistakes.

At the heart of accepting responsibility for one's behavior is the willingness to admit, "I was wrong." Paul J. Meyer, founder of Success Motivation, Inc., and coauthor of *Chicken Soup for the Golden Soul,* said, "One of the most important success factors is the willingness to admit you were wrong."[1] I agree with Spencer Johnson, MD, who said, "Few things are more powerful than having the common sense, wisdom, and strength to admit when you've made a mistake and to set things right."[2] Learning to say "I was wrong" is a major step toward becoming a responsible and successful adult.

"IT'S LIKE HE CAN DO NO WRONG"

Many people need to hear the very words "I was wrong. I accept responsibility" as part of the reconciliation process. Understanding this reality can make all the difference in the world when you sincerely wish to apologize for your behavior.

Joy and Rich were in my office after five years of marriage. Financially, things were going well. Rich had landed a good job upon graduating from college. Joy had worked full-time for the first two years until the baby came. Both sets of in-laws lived in town and were willing babysitters. Therefore, Rich and Joy had been able to enjoy a fair amount of leisure time together. In Joy's words, "Really, our lives are wonderful. The only problem is, Rich is never willing to apologize. When he gets upset because things don't go his way, he lashes out at me in anger. Instead of apologizing, he blames me for his anger. It's like he can do no wrong."

When I turned to Rich, he said, "I don't think it's right to apologize for something when it's not your fault. I do get mad, but it's because she puts me down and makes me feel like I'm not a good father. I spend as much time with our son as I can, but every week she nags me by making remarks such as 'Your son's not going to know you if you don't spend more time with him.' I have to work hard on my job, and when I get home, I'm tired. I need some time to unwind. I can't walk in the house and spend two hours playing with Ethan."

"I've never asked you to spend two hours," Joy answered. "Fifteen minutes would be a good place to start."

"That's what I'm talking about," said Rich. "If I spent fifteen minutes, I'll guarantee you she'd be asking for twenty-five the next week. I can't please her no matter what I do."

It was obvious to me that Joy's comments were striking at Rich's self-esteem. He wanted to be a good father, and her comments suggested that he was a failure. He was unwilling to accept that conclusion, and his way of expressing his hurt was to lash out with angry words. The fact is both Joy and Rich needed to apologize. The problem was that neither thought that he or she had done anything wrong. Neither of them intended to hurt the other. Yet both of them were guilty of treating each other unkindly.

How Rich Grew Up

When I met with Rich alone, it didn't take long to discover why Joy's comments about his needing to spend more time with Ethan had bothered him so much. He grew up in a home where his father was gone most of the time. Usually he left the house on Sunday evenings and returned Friday afternoons. The weekends were spent golfing and watching sports events. Rich had played golf with his father a few times in high school, and occasionally they watched a football game together, but Rich went off to college with a feeling that he really didn't know his father. He vowed that would never happen if he had a child, that he would find a way to connect, that his son would know he was loved.

Rich's angry response mirrored what he had seen his mother do to his dad, lashing out at him. Rich identified with his mother's pain and felt that she was justified in her treatment of his dad. Now as an adult, he felt justified in the harsh but true words he spoke to Joy. So he felt no need to admit wrongdoing.

I tried to help Rich understand that the parental example he had grown up with was not necessarily a healthy model. He readily agreed that his father and mother did not have the loving, caring, supportive marriage he desired. I told him that as long as he followed his parents' model, such a marriage would remain an ideal—not a reality. And I tried to help him see the difference between *understanding* why we do what we do and *accepting* what we do. It was easy to understand why Rich responded the way he did to Joy, but to accept that behavior as appropriate was to destroy the very thing he wanted: an intimate marriage.

The Agree/Disagree Approach

I challenged him to a new approach. It is an approach that has helped many couples live successfully in the world of human failure. I call it "agree/disagree." I *agree* that I have a right to feel hurt, angry, disappointed, and frustrated or whatever else I may be feeling. I don't choose my feelings; I simply experience them. On the other hand, I *disagree* with the idea that because of my feelings, I have the right to hurt someone else with my words or behavior. To hurt my spouse because my spouse has hurt me is like declaring civil war, a war in which there are no winners. Therefore, I will seek to express my emotions in a way that will not be hurtful to my spouse but will hold potential for reconciliation. We worked together on a statement that Rich might deliver that would accomplish this objective. Here's what we came up with:

"Honey, I love you very much and I love Ethan very much. I want more than anything to be a good husband and a good father. Maybe I want it even more because I didn't have a close relationship with my dad, and I saw my folks fight each other all the time. Therefore, I want to share something with you that hurts me very deeply, and I want to ask you to help me find a solution. When I heard you say last night, 'If you don't spend more time with Ethan, he's going to grow up and not know who you are,' I felt a dagger pierce my heart. In fact, I went up to the office and cried because that's the last thing in the world I want to happen. Will you help me work on my schedule so that I can have meaningful time with Ethan and yet be able to work and meet our financial needs?"

I assured Rich that I believed that Joy would respond positively to such a statement. He agreed.

Then I said, "I've worked with people long enough to know that simply having a new plan will not necessarily stop the old patterns. Chances are sometime within the next few weeks, you will revert to your old pattern of lashing out with angry words to Joy when she makes a comment to you. It's not what you want to do, but you will do it before you think. This is when an apology is necessary. I think you will agree that yelling at one's wife is not kind, loving, tender, or positive." Rich was nodding his head. "Therefore, it is wrong."

I reminded him that the New Testament Scriptures challenge husbands to love their wives and care for them, seeking to meet their needs as Christ did for the church.[3]

"Screaming at a wife does not fit the formula for a successful marriage." Rich was nodding again. "Please, I want you to learn to say the words, 'Last night, I lost my temper. I yelled at you and said some pretty nasty things. I was wrong to do that. It was not tender, it was not loving, and it was not kind. I know I hurt you very much, and I'm sorry because I don't want to hurt you. I want to ask you to forgive me. I know I was wrong.'"

Rich wrote the words down in his iPhone. We prayed together and asked God's help as Rich sought to implement his new approach for handling hurt and anger. It was a heavy session, but I felt that Rich was open to change.

Joy's Challenge to Forgive

My session with Joy was more difficult—not because she didn't want to have a better marriage, but because she found it almost impossible to understand how a man could rage at his wife in anger if he really loved her. To her, the two were incompatible. Therefore, she had come to question Rich's love for her.

I expressed empathy for her perspective but tried to help her understand that all of us are imperfect lovers. It is true that perfect love would never hurt the one loved, but none of us are capable of perfect love for one simple reason: we are imperfect. The Bible makes this very clear. We are all sinners.[4] Even those who say they are Christians are still capable of sinning. That is why we must learn to confess our sins to God and to the person we've sinned against.[5] Good marriages are not dependent upon perfection, but they are dependent upon a willingness to acknowledge our wrong and to seek forgiveness.

I could tell that Joy theoretically agreed with what I was saying. She had been brought up in the church, and she knew these realities, but the emotional pain that she had felt from Rich's harsh words made it very difficult for her to forgive him. "Especially when he never apologizes," she said. I agreed with her that an apology was an integral part of forgiveness and reconciliation. I asked her what she expected to hear in a genuine apology. "I want it to be sincere," she said. "I don't want him to just say, 'I'm sorry that you got hurt.' I want him to acknowledge that what he did was wrong. It hurts so badly," she said. "How can he just walk away and never apologize? How could he not realize how wrong it is to scream at someone?"

For the next thirty minutes Joy and I talked about the relationship between hurt and self-esteem. I tried to explain to her the emotional dynamics of Rich's family and why her comments about his not being a good father hurt him so deeply. They may have been true at least from her perspective, but to him, it was like a verbal bomb exploding in his soul. His natural response was to fight back just as he had often seen his mother do.

"Can he change his ways, having grown up with this model?" she asked.

"That's the wonderful thing about being human," I said. "We are capable of change, especially when we reach out for God's help. I believe that Rich is sincere, and I believe that he is beginning to understand himself better. I also believe that you will see significant change in the future," I added.

"I hope so," replied Joy. "I love him so much, and I want us to have a good marriage. I know we're in real trouble. I just hope it's not too late."

We ended our session talking about how Joy might express her own concerns about Rich's spending time with Ethan in a positive way that would not strike at his self-esteem. I suggested that if she would make a specific request of Rich, it would less likely be taken as condemnation. A suggestion or a request is very different from a demand. We explored the kind of things she might request of Rich. Here's part of the list that we came up with.

- "Would you play Chutes and Ladders with Ethan while I finish getting the meal together?"
- "Could the three of us take a walk after dinner?"
- "Could you read Ethan a story while I run his bathwater?"
- "Could you play with Ethan in the sandbox for a few minutes later?"

I could see that Joy was getting the idea of specific requests rather than general complaints. I challenged her, "Never more than one request per week, okay? And when he does things with Ethan, always give him an affirming word. Tell him how proud you are of the good job he is doing as a father. Tell him how much you appreciate him playing with Ethan while you finish the meal. Don't let anything go unnoticed or unaffirmed. Since Rich wants desperately to be a good father, when you affirm him, you are building his self-esteem. And you are creating a positive emotional climate between the two of you."

The next four sessions with Rich and Joy were fully as productive as the first three. It was exciting to see them gain new insights about themselves, recognize their past emotional patterns, and develop new ways of responding to each other. Rich learned to say "I was wrong" when, on occasion, he spoke harshly to Joy. She also learned to say "I was wrong, and I'm sorry I hurt you" when she would slip and make a negative comment about his skills as a father.

It became obvious in the course of our counseling that Rich's primary apology language was "I'm sorry." When Joy said these words, he was ready to forgive her. On the other hand, Joy's primary apology language was "I was wrong." What she wanted to sense was that Rich knew that his angry words were wrong. Their marriage took a giant step forward when she learned to express real regret, and he learned to accept responsibility for his wrong behavior, and they learned to verbalize it to each other.

THE POWER OF "I WAS WRONG"

For many people, the most important part of an apology is acknowledging that one's behavior is wrong. Linda from Seattle said to me, "My husband will not admit that he ever does anything wrong. He just sweeps it under the rug and doesn't want to talk about it anymore. If I bring it up again, he will say, 'I don't know what I did. Why can't you just forget it?' If he could admit that it was wrong, I would be willing to forgive him, but when he acts like he did nothing wrong, it's terribly difficult to overlook it."

As tears came to her eyes, she said, "I just wish I could hear him say one time 'I was wrong.'"

Alyssa is twenty-seven. While growing up, her dad told her that a wise person is willing to accept responsibility for his or her mistakes. "I'll never forget what he said, 'All of us make mistakes, but the only mistake that will destroy you is the one you are unwilling to admit.'

"I remember when I was young and would do something against the rules, he would look at me and ask, 'Do you have something you'd like to say?' He would smile, and I would say, 'I made a mistake. I was wrong. Will you forgive me?' He would give me a hug and say, 'You are forgiven.' Admitting my mistakes is a part of who I am, and I owe it to my father."

Five years ago Alyssa married David, whom she describes as "the most honest man I've ever met." She adds, "I don't mean he's perfect; I mean he is always willing to admit his failures."

"I guess that's why I love David so much, because he has always been willing to say, 'I made a mistake. I was wrong. Will you forgive me?' I like a person who is willing to accept responsibility for his mistakes."

Michael, a twenty-four-year-old single, never heard his father apologize to his mother or to him. At eighteen he left home and has never returned to visit.

"I felt that my father was hypocritical," he explained. "In the community he was recognized as a successful man, but in my mind he was a hypocrite. I guess that's why I have always been quick to apologize, willing to admit my failures. I want my relationships to be real, and I know that can't happen if I'm not willing to admit that I was wrong."

For people like Michael, if you want them to sense the sincerity of your apology, you might use statements like these:

STATEMENTS OF ACCEPTING RESPONSIBILITY

I know that what I did was wrong. I could try to excuse myself, but there is no excuse. Pure and simple, what I did was selfish and wrong.

I made a big mistake. At the time, I didn't think much about what I was doing, but in retrospect, I guess that's the problem. I wish I had thought before I acted. What I did was wrong.

The way I spoke to you was wrong. I spoke out of anger, trying to justify myself. The way I talked to you was unkind and unloving. I hope you will forgive me.

I repeated a mistake that we've discussed before. I really messed up. I know that it was my fault.

TALK ABOUT IT

Name a few of the most outrageous excuses you have heard people claim for refusing to admit wrongdoing. Why do you think these people had such a difficult time admitting a wrongful act?

This chapter teaches that we often believe "To admit that we are wrong is perceived as weakness." How does it make you feel to admit that you were wrong?

When was a time you felt you had done nothing wrong, yet someone expected an apology? How did you respond?

MAKING
RESTITUTION

"How Can I Make It Right?"

MAKING RESTITUTION

It was one of those feel-good stories you see on TV before Christmas. In the Youngstown, Ohio, area, a thief made off with cash from one of those familiar Salvation Army red kettles. In fact, the perpetrator, apparently dressed in a Salvation Army jacket, walked away with the money and the kettle while the bell ringer was taking a break.

But what could have been a sad "stealing from the poor" story turned into something more heartwarming two days later, when someone anonymously left $130 and a note of apology at the Salvation Army's offices. "Here is the money I took plus money for a new kettle and bell . . . Please forgive me."[1]

The unidentified wrongdoer not only apologized—he or she made restitution, making a tangible effort to right the wrong they committed.

The idea of "making things right" to make up for a wrong is embedded within the human psyche, from our judicial system to the arena of family relationships. If Sophia's little brother Jacob steals her favorite toy, Mom or Dad or Grandma makes him give it back. If a criminal steals from someone, a judge orders him to repay his victim in some way. Rather than simply spending time in prison, the criminal needs to make efforts to make up for the wrong to the one who was wronged.

"I EXPECT HIM TO TRY TO REPAIR WHAT HAS GONE WRONG"

The *New Webster's Dictionary* defines *restitution* as "the act of giving back to a rightful owner" or "a giving of something as an equivalent for what has been lost, damaged, etc."

Everett Worthington Jr., professor of psychology at Virginia Commonwealth University and a leader in research on forgiveness, calls the act of making such amends "equalizing."

> Equalizing is making up for the loss that the other person experienced. To offer *restitution* is to equalize the balance of justice. Any hurt or offense causes the person who is hurt to lose something. Perhaps he or she loses self-esteem, self-respect, or a tangible benefit (such as if I offend you in front of your boss and you lose a promotion opportunity). So it is an act of kindness for the transgressor to offer to make up for the loss.[2]

For some people, restitution is their primary apology language. For them the statement, "It is not right for me to have treated you that way," must be followed with, "What can I do to show you that I still care about you?" Without this effort at restitution, this person will question the sincerity of the apology. They will continue to feel unloved even though you may have said, "I'm sorry—I was wrong."

They wait for the tangible reassurance that you genuinely love them.

This reality surfaced again and again in our research. We kept hearing such statements as:

"I expect him to try to repair what has gone wrong."

"I expect her to be truly sorry from the heart and be willing to make things right."

"I want him to make amends as appropriate. Things don't just go away by saying 'I'm sorry.'"

The question, then, is how do we make restitution in the most effective way? Since the heart of restitution is reassuring the spouse or family member that you truly love him or her, it is essential to express restitution in the love language of the other person.

LEARNING THE FIVE LOVE LANGUAGES

After many years of marriage and family counseling, I am convinced that there are fundamentally five emotional love languages. Each person has one of the five as a primary language. If you speak their primary love language, he or she will be reassured of your love, and restitution will be successful. However, if you don't speak the primary love language, your best efforts at apologizing may not be successful. Therefore, let me review briefly the five love languages[3] and illustrate from my research how speaking the primary love language will make your efforts at restitution successful.

Words of Affirmation

Love language number one is *words of affirmation*, using words to affirm the other person. "You look nice in that outfit"; "I really appreciate what you did for me"; "You are so thoughtful"; "Every day I am reminded of how much I love you"; "I really appreciate this meal. You are an excellent cook. I know it takes a lot of time and energy, and I really appreciate it." Using words to affirm the other person may focus on their personality, behavior, dress, accomplishments, or beauty. The important thing is that words communicate verbally your affection and appreciation for the person.

Here are a couple of examples of people for whom words of affirmation is their primary love language and how hearing those words made their spouse's efforts at restitution successful.

Elizabeth is twenty-nine and has been married to Brad for four years. "I know that Brad's apology is sincere when he takes back his thoughtless words and then tells me how much he loves me. Sometimes he goes to the extreme in telling me how wonderful I am and how sorry he is that he hurt me. I guess he knows that it takes a lot of positive words to make up for the things he has said."

Tim met with me during a break at one of my marriage seminars. We had been discussing apologies, and he said of his wife, "She's almost always successful in her apologies. She's the best apologizer I know."

I was impressed, and listened intently as he explained. "She generally says something like, 'Tim, I am so sorry. You are so wonderful and I'm so sorry that I've hurt you. Will you please forgive me?' And then she gives me a hug. It works every time. It's those words 'You are so wonderful' that get me. I've never failed to forgive her because I know she means it. We all make mistakes; I don't expect her to be perfect, but it surely feels good when she tells me how wonderful I am while asking me to forgive her."

For Tim, words of affirmation reflect his primary love language and that's his favorite part of an apology. It's all the restitution he needs.

Acts of Service

A second love language is *acts of service.* This love language is based on the old axiom "Actions speak louder than words." For these people, love is demonstrated by thoughtful acts of kindness. Vacuuming, getting the oil changed in her car, changing the baby's diaper, bringing your spouse a cup of coffee in the morning . . . these are all acts of service.

Gwen was in my office, and she was visibly upset. "I'm sick and tired of his apologies," she said. "'I'm sorry, I'm sorry, I'm sorry.' That's all he ever says. That's supposed to make everything all right. Well, *I'm* sorry, but when he screams and yells at me and calls me names, that doesn't make it all right.

"What I want to know is: Does he still love me, or does he want out of the marriage? If he loves me, then why doesn't he do something to help me around the house? I'm tired of living with a man who sits in front of the TV while I cook the meals and wash the dishes. I work outside the home too. How can he love me and do nothing?"

Obviously, Gwen's primary love language is acts of service, and her husband is not speaking it. Therefore, his apologies fall on deaf ears. She cannot conceive that he could be sincerely sorry and yet fail to love her.

I spent some time with Gwen and explained to her the five love languages and told her that my guess was that her husband had no clue as to what her love language was. And she probably had no idea about his love language. Within three months she and her husband, Mark, had discovered—and were speaking—each other's primary love language. Their marriage was back on track too. He realized that a verbal apology to her was never enough. It had to involve restitution—the reassurance of his love—and this needed to be expressed in acts of service. I don't see Mark often, but when I do, he always thanks me for the insights on love and apology that "saved my marriage."

At the conclusion of my marriage seminars, I typically invite the husband to take his wife's hands, look into her eyes, and repeat after me the following words: "I know I'm not a perfect husband. I hope you will forgive me for past failures. I sincerely want to be a better husband, and I'm asking you to teach me how." Then I ask the wives to repeat similar words to the husbands. One woman, unable to say those words to her husband, later revealed on one of our apology research questionnaires that she could not think of one time her husband made a successful apology during their thirteen-year marriage. She added, "My first hope [of having him truly apologize] was at the end of your conference. I couldn't say the words back to him at that moment, but by that evening, he was helping out with the kids and with dinner. I knew that something had happened to him. I'm hoping he has discovered that acts of service is my love language.

"It remains to be seen if he will continue this change of behavior," she continued. "I know that if I felt like he really loved me, I would be willing to forgive him for everything in the past. More than anything, I want my husband to love me." The success of his apology is now dependent upon him making amends for the past by reassuring his wife that he loves her by speaking her primary love language.

This same principle applies in friendships. Ben was a handsome, intelligent city planner, who ran into a conflict with Steve, another planner in his work group. Initially, Ben and Steve felt that they had a lot in common, and they had enjoyed discussing their shared interests in golf and politics over lunch most days. One day, as a practical joke, Steve commandeered Ben's office computer while Ben was away. Steve pretended to be Ben and sent out an email to their six-person work group, inviting them all to come to Ben's house for a New Year's Eve dinner party: "Don't bring a thing—just yourself!" The next day, a colleague alerted Ben about the counterfeit invitation. Far from being amused, Ben felt angry and betrayed.

When confronted by Ben, Steve could tell that Ben really hadn't appreciated the joke, and he offered a sincere apology. Before Ben could accept the apology, however, he needed Steve to make things right. At Ben's insistence, Steve sent out a correction email to the work group. This retraction allowed Ben to feel that Steve had owned up to the problem he had created and set things right again. Their friendship had a second chance. Had Steve been unwilling to take this action, Ben would have considered his apology incomplete, likely ending their friendship.

Receiving Gifts

A third love language is *receiving gifts*. It is universal to give and receive gifts as an expression of love. Anthropologists have explored the ethnographies of hundreds of cultures around the world. They have never discovered a culture where gift giving is not an expression of love. A gift says, "He was thinking about me. Look what he got for me."

The gifts need not be expensive. Haven't people always said, "It's the thought that counts"? However, it is not the thought left in your head that counts but rather the gift that came out of the thought in your head.

From an early age, children will pick dandelions from the front yard and give them as expressions of love to their mothers. Couples can do the same thing, though I wouldn't suggest dandelions. Even as an adult, you don't have to pay much: If you have no flowers in your yard, try your neighbor's yard. Ask them; they will give you a flower.

For some people, receiving gifts is their primary love language. Therefore, if the person you've offended prefers the love language of *receiving gifts* and you wish to make amends for the wrong you have done, giving gifts will be an effective method of restitution.

Bethany finds her husband's apologies sincere, because he speaks her language. "He makes his apology; then that evening, he brings me a rose to make up for what he has done that has offended me. I don't know what it is, but the rose seems to communicate to me that he is really sincere. So I forgive him."

"How many roses have you received through the years?" I asked.

"Dozens," she answered. "But every time I receive one, it says to me that he still loves me." For her, the gift was restitution.

With their son sick and often in the hospital, Susan tried to understand her husband's tenseness. "A lot of pain and anger was taken out on me, but I let it slide off because I understood. Out of the blue one day, he walked into the hospital room with flowers and a card and a full apology for taking his stress out on me. It was one of the most tender times in our marriage. He realized by his own conviction that he was hurting me, and he took the initiative to apologize. The flowers and the card sealed it for me. I knew he was sincere."

He not only apologized, but he made restitution by speaking Susan's love language, *receiving gifts*.

Quality Time

Love language number four is *quality time*. Giving another person your undivided attention communicates "You are important to me." Quality time means no distractions. The TV is off; the phone is on the table along with the book. You are not paying the bills; you are not cleaning the kitchen. You are giving the other person your undivided attention. If I give my wife twenty minutes of quality time, I have given her twenty minutes of my life, and she has done the same for me. It is a powerful emotional communicator of love.

For some people, this is their primary love language. Nothing communicates love more deeply than quality time. Such times do not even need to include major activities or projects together; they can simply be extended conversations between two people. For those people, quality time is an excellent way to make restitution.

Mary from St. Louis recalls a powerful apology she received the Sunday afternoon after attending the marriage conference. She and her husband had lunch together, and they were beginning to relax when "Phil looked at me and said how sorry he was for how he had been treating me. He was just miserable, and we weren't even talking to each other.

"He looked at me while holding my hands and thanked me for buying the tickets for the conference. He told me that it had opened his eyes and challenged him to be the husband he had neglected to be for the past five years of our marriage.

"Just seeing the true joy and sorrow in his eyes convinced me that he was sincere. The fact that he set aside time to talk to me and to apologize for his actions the past week was almost more than I could believe. In the past every time he tried to apologize, he would say 'I'm sorry,' and that was it. It was like putting catsup on a hotdog; it was just something you always do. This time, it was different. I knew that he was sincere, and I freely forgave him."

Phil was speaking Mary's love language, quality time, and that made all the difference.

You don't have to hold hands, but you do need to give your full attention to the person to whom you are apologizing. If the person you've offended feels loved by having quality time with you, then only quality time will convince them that your apology is sincere. Giving your undivided attention while making the apology is restitution enough. It communicates deeply to the person that he or she is loved.

Physical Touch

Love language number five is *physical touch*. We have long known the emotional power of physical touch. That's why we pick up babies and hold and cuddle them. Long before they understand the meaning of the word *love*, they feel loved by physical touch. The same is true of adults. Holding hands, kissing, embracing, putting an arm around the shoulder, giving a pat on the back, or running your hand through their hair are all expressions of the language of physical touch. We're not only talking about couples. Physical touch is appropriate among all family members, including mothers and sons and fathers and daughters. For some people, this is their primary love language. Nothing speaks more deeply of love than affirming touch. For them, an apology without touch may appear insincere.

Dave and his ten-year-old son, Jake, had gotten into an argument. In the heat of anger, Dave had accused his son of being lazy and irresponsible. Jake began crying uncontrollably. Dave knew that his words had been extremely hurtful to Jake.

"Jake, I'm sorry," he said. "I lost my temper. What I said is wrong. You are not lazy, and you are not irresponsible. You are a ten-year-old boy who loves to play and enjoy life. I should have been more thoughtful about asking you to interrupt your game to do something that I wanted you to do. I love you very much, and it hurts me to know that I have hurt you."

He went over to Jake and gave him a big bear hug. Jake sobbed even more uncontrollably, but this time with great relief. When he regained his composure, his father looked him in the eyes and said, "I love you so much." And Jake said, "I love you too, Dad," as he gave his father a hug around the neck. His father's apology was effective because he made restitution by speaking his son's primary love language, physical touch.

"What do you expect in an apology from your wife?" we asked Judson from Minneapolis, who had been married to his wife for fifteen years. He responded, "I expect her to understand that what she did was very hurtful, say that she is sorry, and then ask for my forgiveness. After granting forgiveness, there has to be a hug for the apology process to be complete."

Judson is clearly revealing that he expects restitution to be a part of the apology process, and physical touch is the language of love he understands best. After the hug, he feels that she has "made amends" for her wrong. Without the hug, the apology process is lacking something important for him.

Marti's illustration of a successful apology indicated how important physical touch was to her. "My husband made a hurtful remark to me in front of the kids. At the time, I reacted and he defended his words. Some days later when we were all at the table, he stood behind me, put his hands on my shoulders, and said in front of our three children that what he had done was wrong and he was sorry and that he wanted to acknowledge it to me and to those who had witnessed it. His apology worked because 1) he admitted he was wrong, 2) he brought healing through his touch, 3) he made his apology public to all who were involved, which made me admire him for teaching his children an important lesson, and 4) for restoring my reputation." The words were important, but it was the affirming touch that "brought healing" and assured her of her husband's love.

If physical touch is one's primary love language, and I want to make a sincere apology, then I must communicate restitution by reaching out to give affirming touches. Words alone will not suffice. It is the touch that makes amends for the wrongs.

REPAYING AND RESTORING

Restitution often extends beyond expressing love through speaking one of the five languages of love. It may require *repayment* or *restoring* something taken—a damaged car, a scratched watch . . . or even a good name. Remember, Marti's good name was restored when Jim publicly acknowledged his "hurtful comment" had taken away his wife's good name among their children. The desire to make amends for one's wrong behavior is a natural part of apologizing if one is indeed sincere.

A Tax Collector Makes Amends

There is a fascinating story recorded in the life of Jesus. The great teacher was passing through the town of Jericho. His fame had preceded Him. In that town lived a tax collector named Zacchaeus. Tax collectors were not the most popular people among the ordinary Jewish populace because they often charged exorbitant taxes for their Roman bosses and pocketed great profit. Zacchaeus wanted to see and hear Jesus, the prophet about whom he had heard so much.

A rather short man, Zacchaeus had a clever strategy. He planned to climb a tree and look down upon Jesus. There he could see and hear, yet go unnoticed by the crowd. However, when Jesus came to the tree, He looked up and said to Zacchaeus, "Come down. I'd like to go to your house for dinner." Zacchaeus was shocked and deeply moved. Apparently he recognized that he was dealing with a man who knew of his self-centered lifestyle and yet was willing to associate with him.

Immediately, Zacchaeus apologized for his wrong behavior through the years and then said that he planned to repay all those from whom he had taken funds unjustly. In fact, he promised to repay them four times as much as he had taken. Jesus interpreted this as the sign of a genuine confession, and He even held up Zacchaeus as an example of how to deal with failure.[4]

A genuine apology will be accompanied by a desire to right the wrongs committed, to make amends for the damage done, and to assure the person that you truly care about him or her. If you are not certain what the offended person might consider proper restitution, you might ask questions like the following:

STATEMENTS OF RESTITUTION

Is there anything I can do to make up for what I have done?

I know I have hurt you deeply, and I feel like I should do something to repay you for the hurt I've caused. Can you give me a suggestion?

I don't feel right just saying "I'm sorry." I want to make up for what I've done. What would you consider appropriate?

I know that I've inconvenienced you. May I give you some of my time to balance things out?

I regret that I've damaged your honor. May I make a (public) correction?

I've broken this promise a million times. Would you like for me to put my commitment to you in writing this time?

TALK ABOUT IT

What do you think of courts offering large sums of money for reparative damages? When do you feel the awarded amounts become excessive?

This chapter suggests there is a voice within us that cries out for those who have wronged us to pay for their act. In what ways has this been true in your life? How have you sensed the need for another person to "pay for" his or her offense against you?

Speaking someone's love language is central in making restitution successful. Of the five love languages (words of affirmation, acts of service, receiving gifts, quality time, and physical touch), which is most important to you? Why do you think this is the case?

PLANNED
CHANGE

"I'll Take Steps to Prevent a Recurrence"

PLANNED CHANGE

Whether we're scanning it spread out over our kitchen table with our coffee or online at the office, we expect our daily paper to tell the truth. Imagine, then, the shock of some Cape Cod, Massachusetts, residents when they read the front-page apology from the publisher of the *Cape Cod Times*. A longtime reporter had simply been making up feature stories. A sharp-eyed editor had gotten suspicious. Databases were searched. Sources were contacted. The conclusion: the people in the stories did not exist and the events described never happened.

So the publisher admitted wrongdoing: "[How] did we allow this to happen? It's a question we cannot satisfactorily answer . . . We must learn from this painful lesson and take steps to keep it from happening again." He then went on to outline exactly what those steps would be.[1]

On the other hand, many couples can identify with the wife who lamented, "We have the same old arguments about the same old things. What upsets me most is not the offending action—it's the *repetition* of the offending action. He apologizes. He promises not to do it again. Then he does it again—'it' being as small as leaving the bathroom light on or as annoying as needless crabbiness.

"I don't want 'sorry.' I want him not to do the thing that bothers me—ever!"

This woman wants her husband to change.

In the context of an apology, planning new steps means that a person realizes that his or her actions are unhelpful, counterproductive, or even destructive. The person regrets the pain he or she is causing others, and is choosing to make lasting improvements.

Planning out specific changes is more than saying "I'm sorry; I was wrong. How can I make this up to you?" It is saying—as the newspaper did—"I'll try not to do this again." For some people, it's a genuine plan for change that convinces others that the apology is sincere. The offending person's new plan that really holds water, then, elicits the offended person's forgiveness.

Without laying out specific steps to prevent a recurrence, the other languages of apology may fall on deaf ears. What people who've been hurt want to know is, "Are you going to take real steps toward change, or will this happen again next week?"

In our research, we asked the question, "What do you expect in an apology?" Repeatedly we heard statements like the following:

"Show that you are willing to change, and do it differently next time."

"I expect them to find ways to stop it from happening again."

"I want them to have a plan for improvement, a plan to succeed and not to fail."

"I expect him not to go into a rage a few minutes later or do the same thing again."

These and scores of similar statements reveal that for many people, true change is at the heart of a sincere apology.

IT BEGINS IN THE HEART

How then do we speak the language of change? *It begins with an expression of intent to prevent a recurrence.* All true change begins in the heart. We recognize that what we have done is wrong, that our actions have hurt the one we love. We don't want to continue this behavior, so we decide that by our own power or with supernatural help, we will change. Then we verbalize this decision to the person we have offended. It is the decision to change that shows something vital in neon letters: we are no longer making excuses. We are not minimizing our behavior but are accepting full responsibility for our actions. When we share our intention to change with the person we have offended, we are communicating to them what is going on inside of us. They get a glimpse of our heart—and this often is the language that convinces them we really do mean what we say.

Abby is thirty-six and thinks her husband, Jeff, is a good apologizer. "What makes you think his apologies are sincere?" I asked.

"Well, he's very honest," she replied. "And what I really like is that he tells me he'll try not to let it happen again. To me this is really important. I don't want to just hear words; I want to see changes. When he indicates that he intends to change, I'm always willing to forgive him."

Tom, fortyish, said, "I expect the person to come to me and sit down face-to-face, not over the phone, and tell me that they were wrong and tell me that they're going to make changes so that it won't happen again. I want them to be realistic and tell me that they know they have to work on it so I should be patient with them."

Some may resist the idea of verbally expressing an intention to change for fear that someone will not actually change. "Won't that simply make things worse?" one man asked me. It is true that changing behavior takes time, and in the process we may have additional failures. (We'll talk about that later in the chapter.) But these failures need not keep us from ultimately making genuine positive changes.

The bigger question is, "What if you fail to verbalize your intention to change?" Your philosophy may be "Just make the changes; don't talk about them." The problem with that approach is that the offended person cannot read your mind. He or she doesn't know that in your heart you have decided to make changes. It may take weeks or months for them to observe the difference in you, but even then they may not know what motivated the transformation. When apologizing, it is far better to state your intention to change. Then the person knows that you truly recognize that your behavior is wrong—and that you fully intend to change that behavior.

It is perfectly fine to tell them that you hope they will be patient with you because you know you will not be 100 percent successful immediately, but that it is your intention to change this destructive behavior. Now they know your intention and sense that your apology is sincere so they can now forgive you even before your changes are fully completed.

"I'll Apologize, but I Won't Change"

Nick is by nature a joker—jovial, always making a humorous comment. The problem is that many of his jokes are off-color. This offends and embarrasses his wife, Teresa. Nick argues, "Hey, they aren't dirty jokes; they're jokes that everyone can identify with. That's why I get so many laughs." However, Teresa is not laughing, and this joking has become a huge issue in their marriage.

Nick is willing to say, "I'm sorry I offended you. It is not my intention to hurt you." But he is not willing to say, "I was wrong, and I will change the kind of jokes I tell."

In my office, he defended himself by saying, "No one else finds my jokes offensive." But by doing a little research we found that a number of people, especially women in his office, found his humor offensive. They had simply not taken the initiative to confront him.

A few weeks later when I shared this information with Nick, he began to think differently. However, it should not have taken this information for Nick to change his behavior. The fact that it deeply hurt his wife and created an emotional barrier between the two of them should have been enough to motivate him to make changes. It was, in fact, his unwillingness to change that had brought the marriage to the point of divorce. When Nick realized he had to change or lose his marriage, he was willing to change.

The idea that we only need to make changes when we are doing something morally wrong is erroneous. In a healthy marriage, we often make changes that have nothing to do with morality but everything to do with building a harmonious marriage. For example, I don't enjoy vacuuming floors, but I do it regularly. I stopped being insensitive to meeting Karolyn's needs when I discovered that her primary love language is acts of service, and that vacuuming floors is a special dialect that she greatly appreciates.

Vacuuming in itself is not a moral issue. It is, however, a *marital* issue and can make the difference between a wife's feeling loved and not feeling loved. I much prefer to live with a wife whose love tank is full. Therefore, my change was a small price to pay for the privilege of living with a happy woman.

BEYOND WORDS—TO REAL CHANGE

The second step down the road of change is developing a plan to prevent a recurrence of the problem. Often apologies fail to be successful in restoring the relationship because there is either no plan for making positive changes, or the plan is not very specific.

Jan and Tom recently marked their silver anniversary, but Jan admits they don't have much of a marriage after twenty-five years: "He has a drinking problem. He often apologizes for the way he treats me when he's drinking, but we both know these are merely words. Words are said in sincerity at the moment, but both of us know that there is no commitment to stand behind the words, no plan for making changes."

Checking himself into a residential treatment center is a plan that could radically change their lifestyle and marriage, but to this point Tom has been unwilling to have a plan to change, so he continues down the same predictable road.

"He's a Good Man, and I Don't Want to Lose Him"

I met Rick and Rita in New Orleans after my lecture on the five love languages. Rick began, "We're having problems in our marriage." He explained that after reading *The 5 Love Languages* a year earlier, he realized his love languages are physical touch and quality time. He told this to Rita and thought her speaking his love languages would help their marriage.

"At the time, I was feeling really unloved by her," Rick said, with

Rita standing at his side. "She spent all of her time with her mother and her friends. I felt like she was married to them more than she was married to me. She told me she was sorry, that she did not want to hurt me, that she loved me very much, and that she would try to speak my love languages, but that was the end of it. Nothing ever changed. It was like we didn't even have the conversation.

"It's a year later, and I still feel like she doesn't care about me or our marriage."

I looked at Rita, who was standing next to him. "I really do love him," she said. "It's just that I didn't grow up in a 'touchy-feely' family and I find it difficult to initiate physical touch. I enjoy spending time with him; it's just that I work full-time, my mother's very demanding, and I like to go out with my girlfriends one evening a week and before I know it, all the time is gone."

"Would you sincerely like to have a better marriage?" I asked Rita.

"I really would," she said. "He's a good man, and I don't want to lose him." In the next five minutes I mapped out a plan for her on how to learn to speak the love language of physical touch. Then I shared some ideas about quality time. I challenged her to sit down with Rick for fifteen minutes on Monday, Wednesday, and Friday nights and discuss their day and how things went. I told her she would find other ideas on how to speak the language of quality time in the book and urged her to read that chapter again.

It was a quick conversation and one that I would have forgotten had it not been for a letter I received six months later. Rick said, "Dr. Chapman, I can't thank you enough for the time you spent with Rita and me at your seminar in New Orleans. It made all the difference in the world. Rita took your plan seriously. She has become extremely fluent in speaking my love languages. I am a happy man and I just wanted you to know that you have made a difference in our marriage." Rita made changes once she had a plan. She had the desire to meet Rick's needs much earlier, but the desire was not turned into reality until she adopted a plan for making changes. Plans need not be elaborate, but they need to be specific.

"I Feared Being Forced to Protect My Child against His Own Father"

Sometimes the offended party will be able to help you work out a plan. A while back I (Jennifer) spoke to a small group of women on the apology languages. A few weeks later I got a call from Carla, one of the ladies who attended. She told me the following story. "My husband, Chad, is a fantastic father, but we all have our moments. One night, he really blew up at our four-year-old son out of his own anger and frustration. My son was pushing all of his hot buttons. My husband did not hurt our son physically, but his rage did scare him terribly. I was so upset that I told him if he ever acted that way again toward either of our children, I would leave him."

Carla and her husband had agreed they'd never threaten each other with leaving, yet she felt anger and dismay over his behavior. "I feared being forced to protect my child against his own father," she explained.

"I told Chad that I needed an apology. He said, 'I'm sorry, but . . .' and then he started talking about our son and how he had made him mad. But I needed him to see how he was 100 percent wrong and responsible in disciplining out of anger. I needed him to see how it scared both our son and me." Carla wanted a plan "so that it would never happen again."

The two worked together on a plan, and the next morning, Chad apologized. "He was so sincere, it made me cry. He also apologized to our son. Our son told him, 'Dad, I was really scared.' My husband's heart broke. He asked, 'Would you forgive Daddy?' My son replied, 'Yes.' Then my husband said, 'I will never do that again.'"

Carla told me that a part of the plan they worked out together was that if her husband felt himself getting angry with the children, he would go to her and say, "I'm getting heated. Will you please take over?" He would take a walk around the block and come back and try to help her in any way he could. "So far the plan is working really well," she said.

PUT IT IN WRITING!

The third step down the road of change is implementing the plan. A plan that is not implemented is like a seed that is not planted. Making the plan work requires thought and action. I have often found it helpful to write on an index card the changes I am trying to implement and to post them on the mirror where I shave in the mornings. It is a way of keeping them on the front burner of my mind. I am more likely to make the improvements if I am consciously aware of what I am trying to do differently today.

Small Changes, Big Difference

Joel's wife, Joyce, was quarrelsome. It seemed to Joel that almost everything she said was negative, and whatever he said, she disagreed with. In our counseling sessions it became obvious to me that for Joyce the world was either black or white. She tended to see everything as good or bad, right or wrong. So, if she disagreed with Joel's idea, his idea was "wrong." It took a while for her to come to understand the difference between something being morally wrong and something being simply a different way of doing or seeing things.

Much of life falls into a nonmoral category. The way one cleans a house or one's taste in restaurants is not a moral issue. It is important to find ways to disagree without being condemning.

Another reality is that people perceive things in different ways. When Joyce realized that her speech patterns came across to Joel as judgmental and affected their marital relationship, she was open to exploring ways of changing those patterns.

One of the plans Joyce developed was that if she disagreed with Joel's idea, she would first give an affirming statement and only then share her opinion. We actually wrote out three affirming statements that she might try.

1. "That's an interesting way to look at it."
2. "I can appreciate that."
3. "One of the things I like about that idea is . . ."

The following week, Joyce admitted that it had been very difficult for her to implement the plan. "I guess I've been in a rut for so long, it's difficult to change," she said. "But by the middle of the week, I was beginning to make the transition. I immediately saw how differently Joel responded. I guess it was seeing the smile on his face and knowing that he was pleased with my efforts that encouraged me to continue working."

She had written the three affirming statements on an index card and read them several times throughout the day. "The card really helped," she said, adding, "I never knew that such a small change would make such a big difference in our relationship."

The Cost of Rebuilding

Sometimes implementing the plan for change can be costly. Caroline came to me (Jennifer) for counseling to help her deal with depression and feelings of betrayal. She had married an attractive professional athlete named Chris when they were each twenty-five years old. Shortly after the birth of their first child, her husband had become involved in an affair. When confronted by Caroline, Chris admitted wrongdoing and said that he wanted to repair the marriage.

During counseling, Caroline and I discussed terms under which she would be willing to work on rebuilding the marriage. For Caroline, it was critical for her to hear from Chris that he was not only sorry for his wrong action but that he would make changes in his lifestyle.

In the end, Chris made a very drastic change. He left the professional sports world and took a desk job in order to avoid temptation. In addition, Chris worked to rebuild Caroline's trust by telling her where he would be and opening up his smartphone and email accounts to his wife.

Caroline needed to know that things would be different in the future, and Chris offered these concessions in order to reestablish trust. Caroline forgave Chris, and five years later, they have a strong marriage.

Julia and Hope were close high school friends who decided to room together when they went off to the same college. In high school, their friendship had been satisfying and comfortable. In college, Julia was quite social, and she busied herself with new activities. Hope, on the other hand, was more introverted, and she wished that Julia would spend more time with her in their shared dormitory room. For her part, Julia noticed that Hope rarely went out except to attend her classes. So she invited her friend to join her in attending a weekly activity with her friends as well as her trips to the gym. Hope consistently refused, saying, "No, because . . ." almost before Julia finished her offer. Hope grew increasingly resentful of Julia's rich social life.

One evening, the lid that Hope had been keeping on her resentment blew off, and in a fit of anger she accused Julia of being a cold, uncaring, self-centered, unavailable, terrible friend and roommate. Julia was quite hurt, and the two lived in near-silence for a few days. To her credit, Hope finally realized that she had been unfair in blaming Julia for her own loneliness. She apologized to her roommate for her unkind words.

Julia wanted to accept the apology—for the sake of harmony in their room, if nothing else. But, she wondered, *Hope has blown up on me once. What if she keeps on doing that?* For Julia, feeling safe in accepting Hope's apology would require a plan for change. The two talked and finally agreed to the following prevention steps: Hope would either join Julia in making friends or find her own way to make new friends. If either of them felt a frustration beginning to build toward the other, they would talk about the issue before they exploded in anger. Finally, they agreed to plan some fun things to do alone together—just like in the old days.

WHAT IF WE FAIL?

Just because we're working on a plan for constructive change does not mean we will immediately be successful. There are often failures along the road even when we are sincerely trying. These failures need not defeat us.

Becky and Josh have been married for four years. She gives this account of what happened in the early months of their marriage: "We had been married for nine months when Josh lost his job, which represented 50 percent of our income. He became depressed, as he was unemployed almost a year. During this period, he threatened to leave me. I knew he was depressed, so I tried not to blame him, but it hurt. He later apologized for threatening to leave me. He said he would try never to say that again.

"He was successful for about a month. Then one day in the heat of anger, he said, 'I'm not good for you, and I may as well leave.' It created a lot of insecurity in me, and I told him how much it hurt me. The next day, he apologized again and told me that he was just so depressed and down on himself, that it was not my fault. He asked me to pray for him, and he hoped never to talk about leaving again.

"He hasn't brought it up again in over three years. In fact, he has a good job, and we're getting along great. I'm glad I didn't abandon him when he was down."

It's better when you can acknowledge any subsequent failure quickly, even before the offended person has time to confront you. A quick apology indicates that you are sincere in your efforts to change. One woman said, "I'm really aware of my tendency to be critical of my twentysomething married daughter, especially when it comes to housekeeping. I'm a neat freak and she is not. My husband actually called me out on my tendency to go over to her house and point out some mess, or bustle around picking up. Otherwise she and I have a wonderful, close relationship, and it bothers me when we bicker. I've apologized and promised to do better, and more than once I've found myself saying, 'Why don't you . . . ' then stopping and declaring, 'No, I am NOT going to nag.' Otherwise known as biting your tongue!"

On the other hand, when we fail to admit our relapses, it communicates to the spouse that we were not sincere in our apology. Due to shame or embarrassment, we usually don't want to admit our failure, but it is better to acknowledge the relapse up front.

Get Up and Try Again

When in our efforts to change we "fall off the wagon," we must admit our failure as quickly as possible. Get up and try again. This is one of the reasons why Alcoholics Anonymous has been so successful in helping people overcome addiction to alcohol. One of the twelve steps is: "Admitted to God, to ourselves, and to another human being the exact nature of our wrongs."[2] Admitting wrong and confessing that wrong to God and another trusted person does require both humility and honesty but gives the opportunity to begin anew.

A while back, I was playing with my young granddaughter. She was trying to build a structure from plastic Legos. It kept falling apart at a certain juncture. I could tell she was getting frustrated with the process, so I said to her, "Let me tell you something that my mother told me. 'If at first you don't succeed, try, try again.' Do you understand what that means?" I asked. She nodded and continued to work on the project.

Later that day, I was trying to open a pickle jar and was having difficulty. She looked up at me and said, "If at first you don't succeed, try, try again." I laughed. She laughed and I tried again, this time successfully. It's an important lesson to learn.

Thomas Edison failed many times before he succeeded in inventing the common lightbulb. Babe Ruth struck out far more often than he hit home runs. Stories abound of famous actors and authors who toiled in obscurity for years, rejected by publishers and overlooked for movie roles, before they found fame. The tragedy is that people often give up when they are next door to success. Old behavior patterns die slowly, but we will be successful if we persevere, prayer-fully committed to change and seeking the support of trusted others to help us through that change.

Inviting the offended person to help you come up with a plan for change is perhaps the best way to effectively show them that you are turning over a new leaf. You might say something like this:

STATEMENTS OF PLANNED CHANGE

I know that my behavior was very painful to you. I don't ever want to do that again. I'm open to any ideas you have on how I might change my behavior.

How could I say that in a different way that would not come across as critical?

I know that what I am doing is not helpful. What would you like to see me change that would make this better for you?

I really do want to change. I know I'm not going to be perfect, but I really want to try to change this behavior. Would you be willing to remind me if I revert to my old patterns? Just say "relapse." I think that will help me to stop and change my direction.

I let you down by making the same mistake again. What would it take for you to begin to rebuild your trust in me?

This is such a long-term pattern for me. While I want to change, I know it will be hard, and I may fail, hurting you again along the way. I would really appreciate it if you would help me think about a way to help my changes stick and encourage me when you see me doing things that help. Can I count on you to be my teammate in this?

TALK ABOUT IT

Name some of the differences you have noticed between men and women when they apologize. Where do you think these differences come from?

This chapter says that all true change begins in the heart. We recognize that what we have done is wrong, that our actions have hurt the one we love. What do you think of this idea? Have you ever seen lasting change begin with an expression of intent to prevent a recurrence?

Talk about a time when you wanted your spouse (or other person close to you) not to just apologize but change their behavior. What happened?

REQUESTING
FORGIVENESS

"Can You Find It in Your Heart . . ."

REQUESTING FORGIVENESS

Years ago my (Jennifer's) mother worked in an office in Chicago where she got along with all her coworkers. But one afternoon a coworker told her she was bothered by the fact that my mother "never apologizes."

My mother hesitated, then remembered an incident in which she had made a mistake that affected this person. "I felt that I had apologized quickly," Mom told me, "taking responsibility and saying that I was sorry for the inconvenience. So I gingerly asked her what she needed to hear from me."

"Well, you never asked me to forgive you!" the coworker exclaimed.

"Well, I want you to forgive me, because I value our relationship," my mother replied. "So let me ask you now, will you please forgive me?"

She responded, "Yes, I will." They both laughed, and things once more were fine between them—because my mother had learned the woman's apology language.

"I KNOW YOU'RE HAVING AN AFFAIR"

When Jennifer told me about this conversation with her mother, I thought of a couple I had counseled several years ago. Angie and Martin had been married nine years when she discovered that he was having an affair with a woman at the office. She confronted him by saying, "I know you're having an affair with Anna. I have eyewitnesses, so there is no need to try to deny it." She gave Martin a choice: either move out of the house within the week or break off the affair and agree to go for counseling. "You can't have both of us. The choice is yours."

Martin left, but within a week, he had come back to say that he wanted to work on the marriage and that he was willing to break off his relationship with Anna. A few weeks into the counseling process, Angie was saying, "The thing that bothers me is that Martin is not willing to ask me to forgive him. He said he's sorry, and I really believe that he has broken off the affair. I would not be willing to work on the marriage if I didn't believe that. But Martin will not ask me to forgive him."

"It's like you are trying to make me say those words," replied Martin.

"I'm not trying to make you do anything," Angie said. "But it seems like you are not willing to admit that you are wrong."

"I *said* it was wrong."

"Then why won't you ask me to forgive you?" she pleaded. "I'm willing to forgive you; I want to forgive you. But how can I forgive you when you don't want to be forgiven? It's as though you don't think you need forgiveness because you haven't really done anything wrong. I don't understand that."

"I know I did wrong," said Martin. "It's just that asking you to forgive me is so hard." He shook his head. Tears came to his eyes and he said, "I don't know why it's so hard!"

In our research, we discovered that there are lots of Angies in the world. When asked, "What do you expect in an apology?" one of every five (20 percent) answered, "I expect him/her to ask for my forgiveness."[1] For them, these were the magic words that indicated sincerity.

So why is requesting forgiveness so important to some people and such a difficult language for others—like Martin—to speak?

WHY SEEK FORGIVENESS?

Why would requesting forgiveness be so important? Here are the answers that we discovered.

First, requesting forgiveness *indicates to some that you want to see the relationship fully restored.* Matt and Kelly have been married for fifteen years. He says, "When she asks me to forgive her, I know she doesn't want to sweep it under the rug. She wants our relationship to be authentic. Whatever else she says in her apology, I know that when she gets to the place where she asks me to forgive her that she is totally sincere. That's why she makes it easy for me to forgive her. I know that she values our relationship more than anything. That makes me feel really good."

When an offense occurs, immediately it creates an emotional barrier between two people. Until that barrier is removed, the relationship cannot go forward. An apology is an attempt to remove the barrier. If you discover that the person's primary apology language is requesting forgiveness, then this is the surest way of removing the barrier. To that person, this is what indicates that you genuinely want to see the relationship restored.

A second reason that requesting forgiveness is important is that it *shows that you realize you have done something wrong*—that you have offended the other person, intentionally or unintentionally. What you said or did may not have been morally wrong. You may even have done or said it in jest. But it offended the other person. He or she now holds it against you. It is an offense that has created a rift between the two of you. In that sense it is wrong, and requesting forgiveness is in order, especially if this is the person's primary apology language. Asking for forgiveness is an admission of guilt. It shows that you know that you deserve condemnation or punishment.

Third, requesting forgiveness *shows that you are willing to put the future of the relationship in the hands of the offended person.* You have admitted your wrong; you have expressed regret; you may have offered to make amends. But now you are saying "Will you forgive me?" You know that you cannot answer that question for that person. It is a choice that he or she must make—to forgive or not to forgive. And the future of the relationship rests on that decision. This takes the control out of your hands, and for some people, this is extremely difficult.

WHAT ARE WE AFRAID OF?

Requesting forgiveness is especially difficult for those people who have strong, controlling personalities. Remember how Martin had so much difficulty in saying the words "Will you please forgive me?" to Angie? When Martin completed a personality test, he and Angie learned he ranked high in the control factor. This means that he felt very uncomfortable when he was not in control of a situation. To ask Angie to forgive him was to relinquish control and put the future of the relationship in her hands. Subconsciously, he found this very difficult.

Eventually Martin realized that the healthy individual is the one who recognizes his/her personality traits, accepts them as being the normal pattern of operation, but refuses to be controlled by these personality traits when they are obviously dysfunctional to a relationship.[2] Therefore, Martin was able to say to Angie, "Will you please forgive me?" She responded with tears, a hug, and a definitive "Yes!" The relationship was restored when he spoke her primary apology language.

Many of us fear rejection, which is another reason it's hard to ask for forgiveness. The fear of rejection is common to humans. Hamilton Beazley, scholar in residence at St. Edward's University in Austin, Texas, and author of *No Regrets*, says, "Apologizing is making an admission that we erred, and we don't like having to do that . . . It makes us vulnerable because we are requesting something—forgiveness—that we think only the other person can grant, and we might be rejected."[3]

None of us like to be rejected, but for some people, rejection is almost unbearable. For such people, requesting forgiveness is really hard because they know that the forgiveness lies in the hand of the other person, and one of the two choices is not to forgive them, which would be rejection.

The answer for this person is to acknowledge this fear—but not to be controlled by it. The reasoning process might go something like this. "I know that my greatest fear is rejection. I also know that my behavior has created a problem in this relationship and that the only way to remove the problem is to sincerely apologize. Therefore, if requesting forgiveness is the apology language of the other person, I will go against my fears and ask, 'Will you please forgive me?'" Mature people recognize their fears but refuse to be held captive by their fears. When they value a relationship, they are willing to go against their fears and take the steps necessary to bring healing to the relationship.

Another fear that sometimes keeps people from requesting forgiveness is the fear of failure. This person typically has a strong moral compass. For them, "doing right" is equated with being good or being successful. Throughout life they have tried to do the right thing. And when they do, they feel successful. To this person, admitting wrong is equivalent to admitting "I'm a failure." Therefore, they find it difficult to admit they are wrong. Typically they will argue vehemently with the other person that what they did is not wrong. They say, "It may have hurt you," or "It may have offended you." "You took it in the wrong way; I didn't mean it that way."

Sometimes the manner in which they defend themselves is more offensive than the original offense, but they don't see this. They will argue, "I'm just trying to get you to understand the truth." It is this kind of person who almost never apologizes. We were not surprised to discover scores of people who said, "My spouse almost never apologizes." One husband said, "She's too stubborn to apologize. We've been married ten years, and I've never received an apology from her." A wife said, "I don't know if it's male pride, but he just can't bring himself to apologize unless I give him the silent treatment for a couple of days. He would prefer that both of us be miserable than to admit he is wrong."

The answer for these people lies in coming to understand that fear of failure—like fear of rejection—is one of the most common fears of humankind! The first step is to acknowledge this fear, first to ourselves, saying something like:

"Sometimes I do and say things that offend someone I love, and it harms our relationship. The only way to amend relationships is by apologizing, so I must learn to apologize in spite of my fear. I understand that making a mistake, saying or doing something that offends another person, is something that all of us do. It does not mean that I am a failure. To admit that what I did was wrong doesn't make me a failure. In fact, it will help me bring healing to my relationship. Therefore, I will go against my fear, admit that I am wrong, and ask forgiveness."

The person who reasons like this is on the road to becoming a good apologizer and a healthy individual.

Lana told her story to us at a conference. "As you began to talk about different apology languages, in my mind I said, 'That's us.' My husband will often say 'I'm sorry' and think he is apologizing. But I will say to him, 'You are not apologizing. You are not saying that you are wrong.'

"As you were talking, I realized we've been speaking different languages. He is saying that he's sorry, and to me that's like it's no big deal. I need for him to ask 'Will you forgive me?' because then it feels like he is admitting his wrong and he is asking me to forgive him. It makes it easier for me to forgive and let the thing go. Before tonight it's like we never had closure whenever one of us hurt the other. We talked about it, and we tried to apologize, but it never seemed to be resolved. Later he would say, 'Well, I said I was sorry. Why are you holding on to this? Why can't you get over it?' I didn't know why I couldn't get over it. It's just that it didn't seem right. Now I get it!"

REQUEST—DON'T DEMAND!

There's a vast difference between *requesting* forgiveness and *demanding* forgiveness. One wife said, "I can hear it now in my head. I've heard it hundreds of times through our twenty-five years of marriage. He insists, 'I said I'm sorry. What more do you want?' I just wish that one time he would look me in the eyes and say, 'Will you please forgive me?' He demands my forgiveness, but he never apologizes, and he never changes anything."

I never had an opportunity to talk with her husband, but I had the strong suspicion that he had a controlling personality and a fear of failure. If these two personality traits could have been dealt with, their relationship would not have ended as it did—in divorce.

Don't demand forgiveness. You cannot expect it. When we demand forgiveness, we fail to understand the nature of forgiveness. Forgiveness is essentially a *choice* to lift the penalty and to let the person back into our lives. It is to pardon the offense so that we might redevelop trust. Forgiveness says, "I care about our relationship. Therefore, I choose to accept your apology and no longer demand justice." It is essentially a gift. A gift that is demanded is no longer a gift.

When, as the offender, I demand to be forgiven, I am like a monarch sitting on a throne, judging the offended person as being guilty of an unforgiving heart. The offended person is hurt and angry over my offense, but I am trying to make her feel guilty for not forgiving me. On the other hand, when I go to the offended party and say, "Will you forgive me?" I am now bowing at her throne and requesting to be forgiven of my offense. I know that if she grants my request, I am a recipient of her mercy, love, and grace. Forgiveness is always to be requested but never demanded.

NOT A SMALL THING

Please understand that when you request to be forgiven, you are making a huge request. It will be costly to the person you have offended. When they forgive you, they must give up their desire for justice. They must relinquish their hurt and anger, their feeling of embarrassment or humiliation. They must give up their feelings of rejection and betrayal. Sometimes, they must live with the consequences of your wrong behavior.

These may be physical consequences that need forgiveness, such as a sexually transmitted disease, a child born of an estranged partner, or the memory of an abortion. Other consequences may be emotional, such as the mental images of your flushed face and raised voice, the images of you in the arms of another lover, or the cutting words that play over again and again in their minds. The person you have hurt must live with all of this and much more, and process it in order to forgive you. This is not a small thing you're asking of him or her. As an ancient Chinese proverb says, "When you bow, bow low."

Because of the costliness of forgiveness, don't expect the offended person to forgive you immediately. If the offense is minor and if you apologize in the primary apology language of the offended person, then perhaps his or her forgiveness may be extended rather quickly. But if the offense is major and often repeated, it will take time for the offended party to process your apology, especially if their apology language is making amends or seeing genuine change. It takes time to observe whether you will follow through on making restitution or changing destructive behaviors. The person must be convinced of your sincerity, and that may well take time.

In the meantime, your greatest virtue must be patience. Be sure you are (1) speaking the person's primary love language and (2) making every effort to change your behavior. If you are consistent in these pursuits, you will likely be the recipient of forgiveness in due time.

Verbally requesting forgiveness *after* you have expressed an apology using some of the other apology languages often is the key that opens the door to the possibility of forgiveness and reconciliation. It may be the one element of your apology that the offended person is waiting to hear. "Will you please forgive me?" is the ingredient that convinces them that you are indeed sincere in your apology. Without the request for forgiveness, your statements—"I'm sorry. I was wrong. I will make it up to you. I'll never do it again"—may sound like glib remarks designed to put the matter behind you without really dealing with it.

Here are some statements that may help you learn to speak the apology language *requesting forgiveness.*

STATEMENTS REQUESTING FORGIVENESS

I'm sorry for the way I spoke to you. I know it was loud and harsh. You didn't deserve that. It was very wrong of me, and I want to ask you to forgive me.

I know that what I did hurt you very deeply. You have every right never to speak to me again, but I am truly sorry for what I did. And I hope that you can find it in your heart to forgive me.

I didn't intend to hurt you but obviously I have. I realize that now, and I see that my actions were wrong even though I was just trying to have fun. It's never right to have fun if someone gets hurt. I promise you I will try never to do that again. And I want to ask you if you will please forgive me.

TALK ABOUT IT

When was a time you thought you had apologized for a situation but later discovered the other person didn't feel that you had apologized? What further action did you take in that situation?

Have you ever had to forgive—or ask for forgiveness? How did you feel?

How can we learn to offer forgiveness even in situations when the other person is unwilling or unable to request it?

THE 5 Apology
LANGUAGES

7

How Do You Say You're Sorry?

Now it's your turn.

As you've gone through the previous chapters, have you recognized your spouse, your child, your friend, yourself in any of the examples? I know that I (Jennifer) have a much deeper understanding of my husband, J.T., through this research. J.T. is a rational thinker for whom debates are routine and being accurate is of primary importance. Recently, I realized that my apologies should include "I was wrong" in order for him to best hear my remorse. He needs me to accept responsibility. In contrast, feelings are my top priority. I need him to express regret, to say that he is concerned about my feelings: "I am sorry." By our thirteenth year of marriage, we had finally learned to shorten our arguments by apologizing not in our own languages but in the primary language of the other person.

What we have learned in our marriage is what Gary and I have found to be true in most marriages: married couples generally do not have the same primary apology language. Consequently, their apologies are often met with resistance rather than forgiveness.

As I looked at our apology survey data from couples, I reviewed the extent that a husband and wife matched in their languages. I found that a full 75 percent of the couples *differed* in their most preferred apology language. Amazingly, of that 75 percent who prefer a different language of apology, in 15 percent of the couples one member's primary apology language was the other member's *last choice*! If you apologize to your spouse in the way that *you* most want to be apologized to, our data suggest that, on average, you wouldn't stumble upon his or her favorite apology language until your third attempt! Assuming the survey is accurate, that means three of every four couples must learn to speak an apology language different than the one they most want to hear!

ASK YOURSELF . . .

Here are several questions to help you identify your own preferred apology language.

Question 1: What Do I Expect the Person to Do or Say?

Randy and Beth were in my office because of an extended argument they had over the fact that he had forgotten their anniversary and had planned nothing special to celebrate it. After listening to both of them for some time, I asked Beth, "What would Randy have to say or do in order for you to forgive him?"

"I want him to say he's sorry," she responded. "I don't think he understands how much this really hurt me. I want him to admit that this was wrong. How could he forget? And it would really be nice if he would try to plan something to make it up to me, something that he would come up with on his own."

"You've mentioned three things," I said. "You want him to tell you that he's sorry. You want him to admit that what he has done is wrong. And you would like for him to do something to make it up to you. If you could only have *one* of those, which would you choose?"

"More than anything, I want him to know how much this has hurt me," Beth said. "I don't think he realizes it. Special days are not as important to him as they are to me."

It was obvious to me that Beth's primary apology language was expressing regret. She wanted to hear Randy say, "I realize how much I hurt you. I know that our anniversary celebration is important to you. I can't believe I forgot it. I'm really sorry." Then if he would throw in "I hope that you will let me make it up to you," that would be icing on the cake and would definitely start the process of forgiveness in her heart and mind.

Question 2: What Hurts Most Deeply about This Situation?

This question is especially helpful if the offender has not yet apologized at all or has not apologized to your satisfaction. Kevin had been hurt deeply by his older brother, Greg. They had always had a close relationship and considered themselves friends as well as brothers. Six months earlier, Greg had gotten a financial tip from one of his buddies at work and had made an investment that had quickly proved successful. He shared his good news with Kevin, and to his surprise, Kevin had gotten angry and said, "I can't believe you didn't let me get in on that! I mean, we're brothers. Why didn't you share that with me?"

"I didn't know that you would want to invest," Greg had responded.

"What do you mean, 'didn't know if I would want to invest'? Anybody would want to invest in a deal like that!" Kevin said. The conversation went from bad to worse and resulted in the brothers not seeing each other for three weeks. Then Greg went to Kevin and tried to apologize, but Kevin did not respond very positively. They started doing things together again, but the relationship was just not the same.

When I ran into both of them at a baseball game, they shared their problem with me. I asked Kevin, "What hurts you most about this whole situation?"

"I think it's that Greg will not admit that what he did was wrong. How could you not let your brother in on a good deal? He said he was sorry, but he won't admit that what he did was wrong."

I looked at Greg and he said, "I don't see it as being wrong. I'm really sorry that I didn't let Kevin know, but I wasn't trying to hurt him. I honestly didn't know that he would want to invest. It was really unintentional."

We talked further and I helped Greg see that even when an offense is not intentional—for example, bumping into someone at work and spilling coffee on him—you would apologize and perhaps help him clean his shirt. "So even though it was unintentional, you would still take the responsibility for your actions by admitting that you should have been watching where you were going, and you would seek to make restitution."

"Yes," Greg answered, "because obviously I spilled the coffee."

I paused for a moment and then said, "Kevin's coffee is spilled, even though you didn't intend it."

"I've got it," he said. "I should have been watching where I was walking the day I got the tip. If so, I would have shared it with my brother because I really love this guy. And I have not enjoyed the last three weeks."

So as I watched the two in the stands of the big ballpark, Greg looked at his brother and said, "I love you, man. And I should have been thinking about you that day. I'll sell the stock and give you half of the profits."

"Hey, you don't need to do that," Kevin said. "You've already done enough. I forgive you."

The two guys hugged each other, and I was glad that I had come to the ball game.

Had I not asked Kevin the question, "What hurt you most about this situation?" I would never have known that his primary apology language was accepting responsibility. So I would not have known how to guide Greg in making a sincere apology. Greg did not have to say the words, "I was wrong." He did have to accept responsibility for his actions by saying, "I should have been thinking about you that day." That's what Kevin needed to hear in order to accept Greg's apology as sincere.

I later learned that Greg did sell the stock and gave half of the capital gains to his brother. That was "the icing on the top of the cake." It would not have been necessary, but it sealed the apology and brought further healing to the relationship.

Question 3: How Do I Apologize to Others?

Usually the language you speak to others is the language you most want to receive. Listen to Mary from Green Bay, Wisconsin: "When I apologize to others, I want to make sure to let them know 'I'm sorry.' I wish it had not happened. I would not want to hurt them in any way, but I realize I have. I want them to know that I'm suffering because I feel very badly that I have hurt them." Mary's own apology language probably is expressing regret.

George is a truck driver from Indianapolis: "When I apologize, I admit that I was wrong. To me, that is what an apology is. If you don't admit that you are wrong, you have not apologized." It's likely George's own apology language is accepting responsibility.

Anna from Charlotte, North Carolina, said, "When I apologize to others, what I try to do is to assure them that with God's help I will not do this again. I want them to know that I am not happy with what I did, and I really want to change my behavior." Anna probably hears an apology best in language #4, planned change, that tries to keep the behavior from happening again.

Perhaps two languages seem to be equally important to you; that is, both speak loudly to you about the sincerity of the other person. When you ask yourself which is more important, you hear yourself say, *Well, really they are equally important.* Then you may be "bilingual," which may actually make it easier for those who seek to apologize to you. If the offender speaks *either* of those two languages, you will sense that he or she is sincere and be inclined to forgive the person.

To further help you in discovering your primary apology language, we have included an apology language profile on pages 177–88. This is not meant to be a scientific instrument, but it is a practical tool to help you discover your apology language and discuss it with the significant people in your life.

WHAT ABOUT THE LANGUAGE OF THOSE YOU LOVE?

But what about discovering the language of a spouse, a child, a parent, a friend? You might encourage them to read this book, answer the three questions given above, or take the profile and discuss it with you. This would be the more overt and probably the most helpful way for the two of you to learn how to apologize to each other effectively.

You could also reframe questions 1–3 and use them to discover the person's primary apology language. You could ask the person to describe an apology that someone once gave him or her that seemed insufficient. In that case, what was lacking? You could ask him, "Was there something the person could have said but chose not to say that would have made your heart feel whole?" Or when you have offended another person, you might ask her: "I know that I have hurt you. I value our relationship. So, what do I need to say or do in order for you to consider forgiving me?" That person's answer will likely reveal her preferred language.

When her husband asked this question, one wife answered, "I'll tell you one thing. I will never consider forgiving you until you admit what you did was wrong. You act like you can say anything you want to say and it's okay as long as you are joking. Well, I'm tired of your 'jokes.' I'm never going to forgive you until you acknowledge that they're hurtful and wrong." Her answer revealed clearly that her primary apology language was accepting responsibility for his behavior and admitting wrong.

When you realize that you have offended another person, you might reframe question 2 to sound something like this: "I know that I have hurt you. I can see it in the way you respond to me. I am sorry. Why don't you tell me what hurts you most about what I said or did?"

The third question can be asked in a more neutral setting at a time when neither of you have recently offended the other. You might say, "I've been reading a book on how to say you're sorry to someone you love. Let me ask you a question and get your opinion. When you express an apology to someone else for something you've done that has hurt them, what do you think is the most important part of the apology?"

If they are open, you share the five apology languages. If they say, "I don't want to hear what's in the book. I'll tell you what's important to me," then listen to their answer and you will likely discover their primary apology language.

William, a fiftyish businessman, was asked this question by a colleague. His response was, "To me, the important part of an apology is letting the other person know that you feel bad that what you have done or failed to do has hurt them." William then recalled a time when he apologized to his daughter for not getting home in time to attend her piano recital.

Seeing her disappointment, he told her, "I realize now how much this meant to you, and I feel really bad that I missed this opportunity to be with you and to watch you perform. I know that you are a great pianist, and I am the loser for not having heard you. I hope that you will forgive me and give me another chance. I love you and your sister and your mom more than anything." He hugged her, and "she cried. I felt that she was trying to forgive me," he told the colleague.

"I felt awful. I tried to communicate that. To me, you are not apologizing if you don't feel awful about what you've done."

This father's answer to his coworker reveals that his primary apology language is expressing regret.

A "10" APOLOGY

But what if you've apologized and you sense that the other person still hasn't fully forgiven you? Here is an approach that may help you deepen the level of forgiveness. A day or two after you have offered your apology, say to the other person, "On a scale of 0–10, how sincere do you feel my apology was the other night?" If the other person says anything less than 10, then you respond, "What could I do to bring it up to a 10?" The answer will give you the practical information you need to continue the apology process until you have done everything possible to pave the way for forgiveness.

One husband asked his wife this question and her answer was, "About 7," to which he responded, "What could I do to bring it up to a 10?" She said, "I mostly believe that you are sincere—but the one thing you didn't say is that you were wrong. I still wonder if you are excusing your behavior because of the way I treated you. I know that I haven't been perfect, but I don't think anything that I have done gave you an excuse to do what you did. I'm not sure that you really feel that."

The husband said, "I can see how you might feel that way. Let me tell you that I know what I did was wrong. There was no excuse for my behavior. I take full responsibility for what I did. In no way was it your fault. I'm sorry that I put you through this, and I hope that in time you will be able to forgive me."

And that, very likely, is just what his wife needed to hear.

TALK ABOUT IT

Which of the five apology languages are most important to you? Think about your closest friend. Which apology language do you think is most important to him or her?

Review the questions for discovering your primary love language. Which one do you find most helpful?

What do you personally desire most in an apology?

THE 5 Apology LANGUAGES

8

What If You Don't Want to Apologize?

I know two brothers who haven't spoken to each other in eighteen years because one brother felt the other took advantage of him in a car-trading deal and the other brother said, "I told you the truth about the car." That happened eighteen years ago, and not a word has been exchanged between the two of them since, even though they live in the same town. How tragic when people make a conscious choice not to apologize.

WHY DON'T PEOPLE APOLOGIZE?

"It's Not Worth the Effort"

Why would people choose not to apologize? Sometimes *they do not value the relationship*. Perhaps they have had run-ins in the past, and a lot of resentment lies buried underneath the surface. As one lady said about her sister, "I gave up on our relationship. It seemed like no matter what I did, it was never enough and I was always in the wrong.

She hurt me on numerous occasions, and I finally decided it wasn't worth the effort. I installed caller ID on my phone so I could identify incoming calls. When she called, I didn't answer the phone. All she ever did was condemn me. It was better not to talk to her. When I go to see my mother, if my sister's car is there, I drive on. I just don't want to get involved."

For a number of perhaps valid reasons, this lady has made the conscious choice to devalue her relationship with her sister. Therefore, she is not motivated to apologize for her own destructive behavior.

"It Was His Fault"

A second reason that people choose not to apologize is that *they feel justified in their behavior; the other person is at fault.* A professional athlete who got involved in a fistfight at a local bar said, "I'm not going to apologize. He shouldn't have made those comments." This athlete's philosophy seems to be, "You do me wrong and you will pay for it. Don't ask me for an apology. You deserved what you got, and don't ever do it again or it will be worse." Obviously, his emphasis was not on building relationships but on exacting revenge. Such an attitude does not remove barriers—it creates them.

This is the infamous tit-for-tat approach to life, and many people practice it. It is in direct contrast to the advice of the Bible, which says, "Do not repay anyone evil for evil. . . . If it is possible, as far as it depends on you, live at peace with everyone. Do not take revenge . . . for it is written, 'It is mine to avenge, I will repay,' says the Lord."[1]

The person who justifies her own wrongful behavior is self-deluded. The man or woman who thinks that he or she never does anything that calls for an apology is living in a dream world. The reality is, all of us sometimes make harsh, critical, and unloving statements, and we sometimes behave in hurtful and destructive ways. The person who refuses to recognize the need for an apology will have a life filled with broken relationships.

We came across this attitude over and over again in our research. Here are some examples of what we heard. Betsy from Birmingham said, "Over a ten-year relationship, I have learned not to expect apologies. I have tried to force/coerce them from him, but they are never genuine and he does not make changes. He says that he never does anything to apologize for. So, I have come to accept the fact that I will never get an apology. I just hope it doesn't continue to get worse."

Martha from Bangor, Maine, said, "My husband is a person of few words. I don't ever remember hearing him apologize. His family never dealt with problems. There are so many hurt emotions in his family and in ours. Things that have been swept under the rug create resentment. As a family, we are just coexisting, because that 'looks' right. I feel like such a hypocrite."

In case you're wondering, this is not just a "guy thing." Women also can refuse to say "I'm sorry." For instance, Jon, who lives in Clovis, New Mexico, said, "Even though I know my wife has done things wrong to me, she always has a way of making me feel guilty. When I think she is about to apologize, the next thing I know, she hasn't apologized for anything but rather has blamed me for her behavior. So I wind up apologizing for her to myself. It's not a very satisfactory apology."

And Mark from Indianapolis said, "My wife never apologizes except when she does something really bad, and even then I don't feel as though she is really sorry."

Often people's consciences have been trained to shift the guilt to someone else. They actually have an *insensitive conscience*, unable to see that the wrong rests with themselves.

Dave's Secret Addiction

Often an insensitive conscience is *coupled with low self-esteem.* Someone may have been taught growing up that apologizing is a sign of weakness. The parents who model this philosophy usually have low self-esteem themselves. They often blame the children for any problems that develop in the family. Consequently, the children develop a sense of low self-esteem and carry this to the next generation. Because they strive so desperately to be a person of worth, and because they see apologizing as a sign of weakness, they too will blame others for any relationship problems that emerge.

People who suffer from low self-esteem, blame-shifting, and a strong aversion to apologizing will almost always need counseling in order to deal with these deeply ingrained patterns of thought, behavior, and emotions.

What these people do not know is this: apologizing *enhances* one's self-esteem. People respect the man and the woman who are willing to take responsibility for their own failures. Receiving the respect and admiration of others thus enhances self-esteem. On the other hand, those who try to hide or excuse wrongful behavior will almost always lose the respect and affirmation of others, thus further compounding the problem of low self-esteem. However, the person who is caught up in this negative cycle will find it difficult to understand this reality.

Dave and his wife, Janet, had suffered several significant losses in their lives. When they arrived for their first counseling session with Jennifer, Dave mentioned that he used to be addicted to pornography but was in recovery from that destructive habit. Janet, of course, felt very hurt, not only by their recent losses but also by Dave's long history of secret addiction.

"Has Dave made an adequate apology for the results of his

pornography addiction?" I asked. Silence followed, and then Dave explained, "Well, I've said that I'm sorry for my addiction, but I didn't go into any detail, because I just thought that the conversation would go badly." Dave was like a mouse that was caught in a trap; he didn't want to jam himself in further by talking about his misdeeds.

I wanted to help Dave see that, ironically, glossing over the pain that he had caused Janet was only going to prolong everyone's suffering. I explained the concept of "balancing the scales" to Dave and Janet: "When Janet learned of your addiction to pornography, it was as if the scales that kept your marriage in balance flew off-kilter. Her side of the scales plunged to the ground. She felt very low, sad, lonely, angry, and afraid of ever trusting you again. Your general apology was unable to bring your marriage back into balance. Janet continues to feel very hurt and scared. If you leave Janet on the low side of the scales, she is likely to unload the weights that are keeping her down by casting barbs at you."

I concluded my analogy by saying, "Janet needs help in removing the weights from her side of the scale. You could do a great service to her and to your marriage by having the detailed conversation that you fear might go badly. Often, people who will give detailed apologies find just the opposite: as they unload the weights of hurt and validate their spouses, they receive gratitude in return. Janet might loosen her hold on the anger that she has been off-loading onto you. She might find your sincere apology to be wonderfully disarming and helpful."

Dave listened carefully. He agreed to try a detailed apology at home and to report back the following week.

They showed up with lightness in their steps. Dave had this to say: "I tried what you said, and it wasn't too bad. I explained to Janet how wrong I was to have kept a stash of pornography in the house all these years. I told her that I was sorry that our kids had found my magazines and that it may have damaged them emotionally. I went into other details—my sorrow over having made Janet feel like an inadequate woman, and my betrayal of her trust when I lied about my activities."

Dave was so pleased with his bold move and the freedom it gave him that he told a male friend to do the same: "I've already explained these unbalanced scales to a friend of mine. He needs to apologize to his wife too, and now he says that he will do it!"

Finally, I turned to Janet. "How did it feel to hear these words from Dave?" She replied, "This was an enormous step for Dave. I had given up on ever hearing him take responsibility for his actions. Now, I am more hopeful about the future of our marriage."

Dave added: "For too long, I believed the lie that 'if we talk more about this problem, it will make the situation worse.' I ignored my conscience and, sadly, I sent the message to my wife that I didn't care about her feelings."

Dave was diagnosed with Stage 4 cancer only four months after his apology to his wife. He now marvels, "What if I hadn't apologized to my wife and dealt with this whole issue while I felt healthy? Please tell your readers that there is a real urgency in apologizing while you still have the opportunity to do so!"

"What If I Can't Learn a New Language?"

A second question we hear often is, "What if the apology language of the other person doesn't come naturally for me?"

It is true that some people will have more difficulty speaking a particular apology language than will others. It all has to do with our history and what we have learned both as children and adults. The good news is all of these apology languages are learnable. We want to introduce you, therefore, to some people who learned to speak an apology language that didn't come naturally for them. Most of them admitted that it was very uncomfortable at first, but they demonstrate the human ability to learn new apology languages.

"I'm Really Sorry I Let Her Down"

James, thinking about marriage, came to one of our seminars with his girlfriend, Serena. After they completed apology questionnaires, Serena told him that the thing she wants to hear most in an apology is "I'm sorry." Later James told me that he didn't know if he'd ever said "those words." He said, "I guess I always thought that real men don't apologize."

"Let me ask you a question," I said. "Have you ever done anything in your whole life that you really regretted? After doing this, did you say to yourself, 'I wish I hadn't done that'?"

He nodded and said, "Yes. I got drunk the night before my mother's funeral. So the next morning, I had a big hangover. I don't remember much about the funeral."

"How did you feel about that?" I asked.

"Really bad," James said. "I really felt like I dishonored my mother. Her death hit me very hard. We had always been close and I could talk with her about things. I guess I was just trying to drown my sorrow, but I had too much to drink. I know that would have made her sad. Mama always talked to me about drinking too much. I was hoping that people in heaven didn't know what was going on here on earth, because I didn't want to hurt her."

"Suppose for a moment that people in heaven do know what's happening on earth, that your mother really was disappointed in your behavior and what you did. And let's suppose that you had a chance to talk with her. What would you say?"

James's eyes moistened, and he said, "I'd tell her that I'm really sorry that I let her down. I shouldn't have gone to the bar. I'd tell her that I really love her and I hope that she would forgive me."

I put my arm on his shoulder and said, "Do you know what you just did?"

"Yeah. I just apologized to my mother. It feels good. Do you think she heard me?" he asked.

"I think she did," I said, "and I think she's forgiven you."

James couldn't speak for a moment. "Oh, man, I didn't mean to cry," he said, wiping tears from his cheeks.

"That's another thing—you were taught that real men don't cry, right?"

"Yeah."

"You've gotten some bad information through the years, James," I said. "Fact is, real men do cry. It's plastic men who don't cry. Real men do apologize. They even say 'I'm sorry' when they realize they've hurt someone they love. You are a real man, James. You've demonstrated it today. Don't ever forget it. If you and Serena get married, you won't be a perfect husband and she won't be a perfect wife. It's not necessary to be perfect in order to have a good marriage. But it is necessary to apologize when you do things that hurt each other. And if saying 'I'm sorry' is Serena's primary apology language, then you will need to learn to speak it."

"Got it!" he said with a smile. "I'm glad we came here."

"So am I," I said as he walked away.

Difficult to Say, Hard to Admit

Marsha has trouble admitting she was wrong—which is exactly what her husband needs to hear as an apology.

"I don't know why," she told me. "Maybe it's because I don't ever remember hearing either of my parents say that, and they didn't teach me how to apologize. They were strong on 'Do your best. Excel. Reach your potential.' But they never said much about apologizing."

About a month after she completed the questionnaire, she left this message on my website: "Lately it's been on my heart to learn to speak my husband's language, so I've been trying. I have actually said out loud, 'I was wrong. I should not have done that.' But it is still difficult to say, and hard to admit. Each syllable felt like glue in my mouth, but it felt good after I said it, like a weight off my shoulders."

Marsha is demonstrating that learning to speak the apology language of the other person is not always easy. She has identified some of the reasons why people find it difficult: It was not modeled by the parents; it was not taught by the parents; in fact, apologizing was not a part of her experience. However, as an adult, she was fully willing to admit that her words and behavior are not always loving and kind. Rather than excusing such behavior, she chose to learn to speak the apology language of her spouse. And it was beginning to make a real difference in the quality of her relationship with her husband.

For those who find it difficult to say the words "I was wrong; I should not have done that," I suggest the following practice. Write the following words on an index card. "I am not perfect. Sometimes I make mistakes. I sometimes say and do things that are painful to others. I know that the other person's primary apology language is hearing me accept responsibility for my behavior by saying, 'I was wrong. I should not have done that.' Therefore, I will learn to say these words."

Read these words aloud. Then repeat the words "I was wrong. I should not have done that" several times alone and aloud in front of the mirror. Breaking the "sound barrier" and saying something you don't feel comfortable saying is the first step in learning to speak the language of accepting responsibility.

Part of learning to accept responsibility for one's behavior is the realization that no one is perfect. I am imperfect and sometimes do and say hurtful things to others. When I choose to admit to myself that I am human and am willing to accept responsibility for the mistakes I make and will apologize using the language of the other person, I am making progress.

"I Might Fail"

Verbalizing one's intent to make real changes—"I will work hard to see that this doesn't happen again"—is difficult for some people. Owen was being very honest with me when he said, "I don't want to promise that I'll change, because I might fail. I really do intend to change, or I wouldn't be apologizing in the first place. But when I say that I'm going to try to change, I'm afraid that I'm setting myself up for failure and it will hurt the relationship even more. Why can't I just demonstrate the change rather than talk about it?"

Owen is expressing the sentiment of many. However, the problem of not verbalizing your intention is that the other person cannot read your mind. You know that you are trying to change, but he or she doesn't know. In a very real sense, we verbalize the intention to change for the same reason that we verbalize the other apology languages. We want the other person to know that we recognize that we have offended them, we value our relationship, and we would like to be forgiven.

Allyson in Mobile, Alabama, expressed it this way: "My husband doesn't see a lot of merit in actually saying the words 'I'm sorry,' 'I was wrong,' or 'Will you forgive me?' or 'I'll try not to do that again.' But when he does not express the words, I can only assume that he isn't sorry, doesn't realize that he has done wrong, and doesn't intend to change. Even if he is sorry and really is trying to change, I don't know that. Without the words, how do I know that you have really apologized? How do I know that you are really trying to change? For me, seeing a plan for change is my primary apology language, and if I know that my husband is at least trying to change, I'm willing to forgive him. But if he doesn't tell me, then it's like he is not speaking my apology language, and I have a hard time believing that he is sincere."

Allyson is making it clear that expressing the intention to change is the first step in speaking the apology language of planned change.

I am not suggesting that you promise that you will never do it again. What you are expressing is that you are going to make every effort not to repeat this behavior. It is effort that leads to success. Changing long-standing patterns of behavior can be difficult. But the first step is deciding that they need to be changed, and with the help of God, you will start walking down the road toward positive change. Most people will be encouraged by your efforts and will be willing to forgive you when you stumble along the road if you are willing to confess the failure.

Don't allow the fear of failure to keep you from taking the first steps down the road of successful changes. If this is the other person's primary apology language, nothing will take the place of the words "I'm really going to try hard to change this behavior." Then developing a plan and following that plan leads you further down the road to success and the healing of past hurts.

CAN YOU APOLOGIZE TOO MUCH?

We have found that there are some people who apologize almost daily. Anytime there was any sense of tension between them and another person, they immediately apologized.

"I Shoot Myself in the Foot"

People who tend to be overly apologetic do so for differing reasons. Some people apologize frequently because they are frequently guilty of words or actions that inflict pain on others. Jeremy told me, "I have more experience apologizing than my wife does because I'm constantly shooting myself in the foot. I'm a rather talkative person. And sometimes that gets me in trouble. I say things without thinking and later realize that I have hurt my wife or someone at work. So I do a lot of apologizing."

Emma says her husband, Andrew, apologizes regularly for a similar reason: "He does something to apologize for every day."

I thought at first she might be joking, but I didn't see a smile on her face. So I said, "You're serious, aren't you?"

She said, "Yes. I never met a man who was so insensitive. But he's quick to apologize. I just wish he could learn to stop doing things he has to apologize for."

For people like Jeremy and Andrew, the problem does not lie in an unwillingness to apologize but rather in a deficiency in relationship skills. They have learned to cope with this deficiency by frequently and freely apologizing. A more satisfying and long-term answer would be for these people to attend classes on how to build better relationship skills, go for counseling, and/or read books on the fundamentals of relating positively to other people.

"I ASSUME IT'S MY FAULT"

Others who tend to overly apologize are suffering from low self-esteem. Lucy is a thirty-five-year-old single who said, "I usually feel as if everything is my fault—at work, at home, and in all of my relationships. I guess I never felt very good about myself. So when things go wrong in relationships, I just assume it is my fault. So I apologize. People often say to me, 'You don't need to apologize for that. You didn't do anything wrong.' But I always feel like I am in error."

Patricia lives in Phoenix. She and her husband retired early and moved from Michigan to a warmer climate. She said about her husband, "Dave constantly apologizes by saying 'I'm sorry.' But it is with the attitude 'I know I'm worthless and I can't do anything right.' Obviously, he is not worthless. He is a great businessman; otherwise, we would not have been able to retire early. And he doesn't do a lot of things that call for an apology. I think it is probably just low self-esteem on his part. But it takes away from the apology."

I never had an opportunity to talk with her husband, Dave, but I had the sense that he was either suffering from low self-esteem derived from his childhood experience or that his excessive apologies were his way of responding to an overly critical wife who had found fault with him through the years, and his way of coping was simply by accepting the condemnation. In either scenario, he was suffering from a self-esteem problem. The road to a better relationship would likely lead through a counselor's office where Dave could deal with his self-perceptions and come to a new and more positive understanding of who he is. He was locked into a pattern of low self-esteem that did not need to continue for the rest of his life.

"I Want to Get It Over With"

Many people are conflict-averse and want to get an issue settled quickly so that things can "get back to normal." They are willing to accept responsibility and apologize even if they do not sense that they are at fault simply to get the issue settled. They don't like the emotional discomfort that comes from long discussions about the issue. They would much rather apologize, accept the responsibility, and hope that they can move on. Here are some examples from our research of people who fall into this category.

"If I want to sleep, then I have to get it over with," says Maria, married to Hector for twenty years. "I find that I apologize [to Hector] even when I'm not in the wrong, just so I can end the fight and wake up with a clean conscience."

John is from New York City and was attending a marriage enrichment event that I was leading. He said, "My parents were nonconfrontational when I was growing up. I'm not used to seeing disputes. So when I get upset or disappointed, I feel I have to apologize and set things right. I grew up Catholic, and I loved the sacrament of confession. I just felt good about confessing aloud and being forgiven."

Jonathan is thirty, has been married for two years, and really enjoys his job. "I don't always have to win, and I don't like confrontation. I will apologize even if it is not my fault because I want to move on. I don't want to waste time arguing. I guess I'm a lover, not a fighter."

Interestingly, several people told me the "best apologizer" was the one who apologized the most—even if the apologizer was not at fault. When I asked Suzanne, "Who is the best apologizer, you or your husband?" she said, "My husband is by far the best apologizer in our marriage. In fact, I would say that he apologizes 90 percent of the time, even when it is not his fault. He wants peace between us, so he is usually the one to make up first."

A "Peace" That Leads to Resentment

For these and thousands of others like them, they desire peace at any price. They would rather admit wrong if the arguments and conflicts will cease. Emotional calm is more important than being right. While this may appear to be an admirable trait, it often simmers as inner resentment.

Kim and Garrett have been married for fifteen years and live just outside Williamsburg, Virginia. She said, "I'm the one who seems to apologize most in our marriage. Garrett is not good at verbalizing his feelings. And in order to get past whatever it is that went wrong and caused hard feelings, I usually end up apologizing just so we can get back on speaking terms again. I often end up internalizing hard feelings because I have to apologize, even when I'm not the one who caused the problem."

Such internalized resentment often creates emotional distance between people. On the surface things seem to be relatively calm, but underneath an emotional explosion is in the making.

If a person senses such emotional resentment building, it is time to talk to a counselor, pastor, or trusted friend. Failure to process the resentment can lead to the destruction of a relationship. Peace at any price is not the road to authentic relationships.

TALK ABOUT IT

When was a time you chose to wait to apologize rather than doing it immediately? How did this affect the relationship?

"Why should I apologize when she's the one who started it?" said the man in the chapter. What would you say to him?

Many people form an "insensitive conscience" over time and no longer consider what they do as being wrong. How have you experienced this in your own life? In the lives of those close to you?

THE 5 Apology
LANGUAGES

9

Learning to Forgive

In this chapter, we move from *making* an apology to *accepting* the apology. As we've seen, forgiving someone for wrong behavior can be tough, especially if we consider the offense to be major.

Let's be clear: the need for forgiveness always begins with an offense. The International Forgiveness Institute, founded by Professor Robert Enright, a pioneer in "forgiveness" research, defines forgiveness as a moral issue: Forgiveness "is a response to an injustice (a moral wrong)," and "it is a turning to the 'good' in the face of wrongdoing."[1] If no offense has been committed, then forgiveness is a nonissue.

All sincere apologies have the same two goals: that the offender be forgiven and the relationship be reconciled. When forgiveness and reconciliation occur, the relationship can continue to grow.

"HOW COULD THEY LOVE ME AND DO THAT?"

Even a minor offense can be like a thunderstorm ruining a picnic. It destroys the tranquility of the relationship. If you're the one offended, you know how it feels: there's hurt, anger, disappointment, disbelief, a sense of betrayal and rejection. Whether the offender is a coworker, roommate, parent, or spouse, the question is, "How could they love me and say or do that?" Your love tank has just suffered a rupture.

There's more fallout: Your sense of justice has been violated. It's like little moral soldiers inside you stand up and say, "That's not right. We will fight for you." Everything in you wants to say to those little soldiers, "Charge!" But you are not sure that is the right thing to do. You value this relationship. You think, *Maybe they didn't mean it like it sounded,* or *Maybe I didn't get the full story.*

Reason prevails as you try to gain information. Perhaps you find that you were mistaken. You read the situation incorrectly. So, your anger subsides and you continue to develop the relationship. On the other hand, investigation may confirm your worst fears. It is real, and it is worse than you thought. The person has wronged you. He has hurt you; she has humiliated you. Her words were unkind, unloving, and disrespectful. The offense now sits as an emotional barrier between the two of you.

Often the situation is compounded by our response. She screamed at you, so you scream at her. She pushed you, so you push her. She said something disrespectful to you, so you reciprocate. Now you are both guilty of an offense. Unless each of you chooses to apologize and each of you chooses to forgive, the emotional barrier will never be completely removed.

Because we are all imperfect, we sometimes fail to treat each other with love, dignity, and respect; apologies and forgiveness therefore are essential elements to healthy relationships. Who apologizes first is unimportant. *That* each of you apologizes is all-important. An apology reaches out for forgiveness. So let's look at the art of forgiving.

What Is Forgiveness?

First, let's clarify the meaning of the word *forgiveness.* Three Hebrew words and four Greek words are translated *forgive* in the English Scriptures. They are basic synonyms with slightly varying shades of meaning. The key ideas are "to cover; to take away; to pardon; and to be gracious to."

The most common of these is the idea of taking away one's sins (failures). For example, the psalmist says, "As far as the east is from the west, so far has he removed our transgressions from us."[2] This psalmist is speaking of God's forgiveness; thus, God's forgiveness is relieving the person from God's judgment—from the penalty due the person who transgresses God's law. Again the Scriptures say, "He does not treat us as our sins deserve or repay us according to our iniquities."[3] Isaiah the prophet spoke of God "blotting out" our sins and remembering them no more.[4] Clearly, God's forgiveness means that our sins no longer stand as a barrier between us and God. Forgiveness removes the distance and allows us open fellowship with God.

The same is true in human forgiveness. Forgiveness means we choose to lift the penalty, to pardon the offender. It means letting go of the offense and welcoming the offender back into your life. Forgiveness is not a feeling but a decision. It is the decision to continue growing in the relationship by removing the barrier.

If you're the offended party, forgiveness means that you will not seek revenge, that you will not demand justice, that you will not let the offense stand between the two of you. Forgiveness results in reconciliation. This does not mean that trust is immediately restored. We will talk about that later. Reconciliation means that the two of you have put the issue behind you and are now facing the future together.

THE FORGIVENESS CYCLE

An apology is an important part of *the forgiveness cycle*. An offense is committed; an apology is made; and forgiveness is given.

Forgiveness Offered Freely

Again, this cycle is clearly seen in God's relationship with people. The prophet Isaiah delivered this message to ancient Israel. "Your iniquities have separated you from your God; your sins have hidden his face from you, so that he will not hear."[5] We are never separated from God's love, but our disobedience does separate us from His fellowship. The New Testament reminds us that "the wages of sin is death."[6] Death is the ultimate picture of separation. Of course, this is not what God desires for His creatures. Therefore, the writer quickly adds that "the gift of God is eternal life in Christ Jesus our Lord."[7] God desires fellowship with His creatures; that is what the cross of Christ is all about. God offers His forgiveness freely.

The Christian message is that in order to experience God's forgiveness, people must respond by deep change *or repentance* (a turning around) and faith in Christ.[8] The message is clear. If we would receive God's forgiveness, we must acknowledge our sin and accept His forgiveness. John the apostle writes, "If we confess our sins, [God] is faithful and just and will forgive us our sins."[9] Thus, in order for our fellowship with God to be restored, we must acknowledge our sin—that is, apologize. The moment we do this, we experience the warm embrace of our heavenly Father. The distance is gone. We are again walking in fellowship with God.

I have taken time to review God's forgiveness toward us because the Scriptures say that we as humans are to forgive each other as God forgives us.[10] That's the divine model, and it is a wise and prudent model for making an apology in today's world. It has two essential elements: (1) confession and repentance on the part of the offender, and (2) forgiveness on the part of the one sinned against.

In the Scriptures, these two are never separated. Therefore, on the human level, the apology is a critical element in the cycle of forgiveness. That is why we have spent the first half of this book talking about how to apologize effectively. However, once the apology is made, the offended person then has a choice: to forgive or not to forgive. To forgive opens the door to reconciliation between the two of you. Not to forgive leads to further deterioration of the relationship.

Jesus declared to His followers, "Do to others what you would have them do to you, for this sums up the Law and the Prophets."[11] Most of us would like to have forgiveness when we fail. Therefore, we are encouraged to extend forgiveness to those who offend us. The Christian message is that we can forgive because we have been forgiven by God. God forgives us because Christ paid the ultimate penalty for our failures. Therefore, our capacity to forgive others comes from God. It is always proper to pray, "Lord, help me to forgive."

When No Apology Is Offered

What if the person who offended me does not come back to apologize? Then I am to lovingly confront the offender. This approach was laid out clearly by Jesus. "If your brother sins against you, rebuke him; and if he repents, forgive him. And if he sins against you seven times in a day, and seven times in a day returns to you, saying, 'I repent,' you shall forgive him."[12] The pattern is clear. An offense is committed. The person does not immediately apologize. So you confront the offender, looking for an apology. If the person apologizes, then you forgive. There is to be no limit to our forgiveness so long as the offender returns to apologize.

What if the offender refuses to apologize—even when confronted with his/her wrong behavior? We are to approach the person a second time, telling them of the offense and giving them an opportunity to apologize. Again, Jesus gave clear instructions to His followers. "If your brother sins against you, go and tell him his fault between you and him alone. If he hears you, you have gained your brother. But if he will not hear, take with you one or two more."[13]

Again, the pattern is clear. You approach the person a second or even a third time. Each time you are willing to forgive and are seeking reconciliation. Ultimately, the offender may be unwilling to acknowledge the need for forgiveness and refuse to apologize for the wrong behavior. Even then, the Christian is to pray for them, seek to communicate the love of Christ, and hope that they will repent of their wrongdoing and experience forgiveness.

Please notice carefully that Jesus did not say we should forgive the offender when he or she is unwilling to apologize. Notice also that Jesus was addressing the issue of moral sin—"If your brother sins against you." Some of our irritations in relationships are simply that—irritations. Our spouse doesn't load the dishwasher the way we do. We may request change, but if our spouse does not, it is not a moral failure. Many of the irritations in relationships we can overlook, forbear, accept. But moral failures always stand as a barrier that can be removed only by apologizing and asking forgiveness.

Therefore, if a person refuses to apologize for a moral failure after being confronted several times, we are to release the person who has sinned against us to God, letting God take care of the person rather than insisting that we pay back the person for the wrongful action. The Scriptures teach that vengeance belongs to God, not to man.[14] The reason for this is that God alone knows everything about the other person, not only his actions but his motives—and God alone is the ultimate judge.

Releasing the Person to God

So the person who is feeling hurt and angry toward another who has treated him unfairly is to release that person to an all-knowing heavenly Father who is fully capable of doing what is just and right toward that person.

Jesus Himself gave us the model. The apostle Peter said of Jesus, "When they hurled their insults at him, he did not retaliate; when he suffered, he made no threats. Instead, he entrusted himself to him who judges justly."[15] Or as another translation reads, He "left His wrongs in the hands of the righteous Judge."[16] As a man, Jesus did not take revenge on those who had wronged Him; rather, He committed the whole situation to God, knowing that God would judge righteously.

Often when we have been wronged, we think that if we don't press the issue and demand justice, then no one will. You can turn your erring friend and the wrong committed against you over to God, knowing that He will take the best possible action on your behalf. He is more concerned about righteousness than you are.

Once you have released the person to God, then it is time to confess your own sin. Remember, hurt and anger are not sinful. But often we allow anger to lead us to sinful behavior. Explosive words or destructive behavior must be acknowledged to God and to the person you sinned against. Don't allow the other person's refusal to apologize to keep you from apologizing. He or she may or may not forgive you, but when you have apologized, you will be able to look at yourself in the mirror, knowing that you are willing to admit your failures.

FORGIVING WHEN THE APOLOGIZER DOESN'T SPEAK YOUR LANGUAGE

I remember the mother who said, "After I heard you speak about the five languages of an apology, it was much easier for me to forgive my adult son. He is thirty years old, and he has apologized many times. But all he ever says is 'I'm sorry.' To him, that is an apology. To me, that leaves a lot to be desired. I want to hear him say, 'I was wrong; will you please forgive me?' But he always stops with 'I'm sorry.'

"In the past, I've forgiven him most of the time. But I always had questions about his sincerity. After your lecture, I realized that he was sincere, that he was speaking his apology language. And even though it was not mine, I believe he was sincere. So it made it easier for me to genuinely forgive him."

THE DANGER OF FORGIVING TOO EASILY

Some of us have been trained since childhood to forgive quickly and freely. If a person makes an apology using any of the apology languages, we are likely to forgive him and not question his sincerity. In so doing, we may end up encouraging destructive behavior.

Lisa and her husband, Ben, faced what she called "many stressors" in their first year of marriage: moving to a new city, selling one house and buying another—twice. Lisa had ongoing health problems; Ben had a new job, his parents separated, and his father threatened to commit suicide; and together the two started a singles' ministry in their church. In Lisa's letter to me (Jennifer), she described the final major setback: "Last, my husband committed adultery."

I read Lisa's letter closely: "I felt God instructed me to forgive him and love him. I did. I reasoned that after all that we had been through, anyone could make a mistake. I freely gave my forgiveness and spoke of this affair only two more times. However, a year later he cheated with another woman. This time I gave him a hard time, and some consequences were handed out. My pastor got involved. We both showed him love and mercy, and I forgave him after he said he was sorry and 'repented.'

"Eight years went by and, unknown to me, my husband continued his affairs. An awakening phone call came from him, saying, 'I am in love with another woman, and I'm not coming home tonight.' At that point, I changed all the locks and had him in the lawyer's office signing separation papers."

Lisa and Ben had a year's separation. During that time, they began to repair their wounded marriage. "By a miracle of God, much counseling, and setting more healthy boundaries, we are affair free—and celebrating fourteen years of marriage," she said.

Yes, that is an amazing ending, and Lisa would say God was in the saving of their shaky marriage. Still, she has regrets that Ben's deception continued as long as it did and that she had not taken stronger action sooner. "I believe if I had known about the five languages of apology and had been a better judge of sincerity, my boundaries would have been stronger earlier in the marriage. I would have been less codependent and weak in the name of forgiveness. My discernment of true change would have been enhanced, and it might have saved us many years of unbearable sorrow."

I think Lisa is right. Holding someone accountable for negative behavior is an act of love. Had Lisa understood the five languages of apology, she likely would have had the courage to say after the first offense, "I love you too much to take this lightly. I will not continue in this relationship unless we can agree to get extensive counseling. Our relationship is too important to me to treat this as a light offense." In major moral failures, we must deal with the cause of the behavior if we expect there to be genuine, long-term change.

"I NEED SOME TIME"

Earlier we indicated that there are two common responses to an apology: to forgive or not to forgive. In reality, there is a third possible response: "Give me some time to think about it. I want to forgive you, but I've got to have some time to process all of this."

Sometimes we have been hurt so deeply or so often that we cannot bring ourselves emotionally, spiritually, or physically to the point of genuinely extending forgiveness. We need time for inner healing, time for the restoration of emotional balance or even physical health that will give us the capacity to forgive. I remember the husband who said, "After my wife's first lie about her drug use, I chose to forgive her and to work on our marriage because I thought she truly regretted what she had done. I was convinced that she would never do it again. But now, she has done it again and again. She entered a treatment program but left three weeks before the program was over. She said she could make it on her own. Well, she didn't. Within a week, she was stoned again.

"This time she is asking me for another chance. She says she will stick with the program. I've agreed to pay for the treatment, but I don't know if I can forgive her. I'm overwhelmed. I'm willing to pray about it, but right now I don't want to see her."

I felt great empathy for this husband. Who would not understand his reluctance to forgive? Who would be so callous as to demand that he forgive her on the spot? Who can give him the assurance that her apology is sincere? And who can assure him that it will never happen again? All the evidence seems to point in the opposite direction.

"I love my wife," he said, "and she says that she loves me. But how can that be? How can you do this if you love someone? It's a strange way to show love. I hope in time that I can forgive her. I hope that she is sincere. I hope that she has realized that she has been walking the wrong road. But right now, I don't know."

This is a husband who deep within wants to forgive his wife. He wants to have a genuinely loving relationship, but he doesn't know if he can forgive her. Time will tell. He is open to the possibility, and he is praying and waiting. Sometimes, this is the only realistic approach to forgiveness. In the meantime, he must process his emotions with God and not allow his hurt to turn into bitterness and hatred.

TRUST: THE TENDER PLANT

This brings us to the issue of rebuilding trust. Forgiveness and trust are not to be equated. Because forgiveness is a decision, it can be extended immediately when one perceives he has heard a sincere apology. However, trust is not a *decision*—it is rather an *emotion*. Trust is that gut-level confidence that you will do what you say you will do.

Obviously, trust has a cognitive aspect: "I choose to believe that you are a person of integrity" is a statement based on trust. However, this statement is rooted in the soil of emotions. Trust is that emotional sense that I can relax with you and don't have to be suspicious. I can let down my emotional guard because you will not knowingly hurt me.

In most relationships, trust develops in the early stages of the relationship. Unless we have been deeply hurt in the past, we tend to assume that people are who they claim to be. If in the early months of the relationship we find no occasion to doubt that, then our initial trust is affirmed and deepened.

Trust, then, is one's normal emotional state in healthy relationships. Friends trust each other. Spouses trust each other. Close vocational associates usually trust each other. However, when trust is violated or betrayed, it does not spring back immediately after an apology and the extending of forgiveness. Trust is diminished because the person proved to be untrustworthy. If I am honest, I will likely say, "I forgive you because I believe you are sincere in your apology. But to be very honest, I don't trust you as deeply as I did before."

I like to visualize trust as a tender plant. When trust is violated, it is as though someone stepped on the plant and pushed it into the mud. The rain and the sun may eventually enable the plant to stand erect again, but it will not happen overnight. So how do we rebuild trust in a relationship when it has been violated? The answer is by being trustworthy one day at a time. A sincere apology and genuine forgiveness open the door to the possibility of trust growing again. How does this happen? In my experience in working with couples through the years, it is fostered best when the offender chooses to open his/her private life to the scrutiny of the offended spouse.

For example, if the offense was in the area of money, then the attitude will be "Here is the checkbook; here is the savings account; here are the stockholdings. You may look at these anytime you wish. I have no other accounts. I will introduce you to the people who manage these accounts and let them know that you have total access."

If the offense was in the area of sexual unfaithfulness, then you allow the partner full access to your cell phone, computer, and any other means of communication. You give a full accounting of all of your time. And you give your spouse permission to make phone calls to affirm that you are where you said you would be. Trust is not fostered by secretiveness but by openness. If you choose to be trustworthy over a period of time, your spouse will likely come to trust you again. If you continue to be untrustworthy by lying, cheating, hiding, and making excuses, trust will never be reborn. Trust's only hope of survival is the rain and sunshine of integrity.

Because the rebuilding of trust is a process and takes time, people have sometimes said to me, "I think I've forgiven my spouse. But some days I feel like I haven't, because I really don't trust them." Their struggle comes because they are confusing forgiveness and trust. In summary, forgiveness is a choice to lift the penalty and allow the person back into your life so that the relationship can continue to grow. Trust, on the other hand, returns in stages. When there is changed behavior over a period of time, you begin to feel more comfortable and optimistic about the other person. If this continues, eventually you will come to trust them fully again.

COMPLETING THE CYCLE

Forgiveness holds the power to give renewed life to the relationship. The choice not to forgive pronounces the death penalty upon the relationship. Without forgiveness, relationships die. With forgiveness, relationships have the potential for becoming vibrant and enriching the lives of the people involved.

It would be hard to overestimate the power of forgiveness. It is the goal of every sincere apology. If forgiveness is not extended, then the apology hangs as a loose electrical wire disconnected from the system. An apology alone cannot restore relationships. An apology is a request for forgiveness. It is the gift of forgiveness that ultimately restores the relationship. If we are friends and you violate our friendship by treating me unfairly but quickly come to me with a sincere apology, the future of our relationship is neither determined by your offense nor by your apology but by my willingness or unwillingness to forgive you. Forgiveness completes the cycle and leads to reconciliation. Without forgiveness, the purpose of the apology is thwarted.

WHAT FORGIVENESS CAN'T DO

Let me be quick to add that forgiveness does not remove all the results of failure. If a man is given to fits of anger and strikes out at his wife, hitting her on the chin and breaking her jaw, he may sincerely confess and she may genuinely forgive. But her jaw is still broken and may cause her difficulty for years to come. If a teenage girl, in spite of her parents' urging, succumbs to trying a popular drug at the request of a friend and that drug adversely affects her mental capacity, the friend, who offered the drug, may apologize sincerely and profusely. The girl may apologize to her parents if she has the mental capacity to do so. The parents may genuinely forgive, but the mental capacity of the young girl is forever impaired.

It is one of the fundamental realities of life: When we commit actions or speak words that are detrimental to another, the consequences of those actions and words are never fully removed, even with genuine forgiveness.

The second reality is that forgiveness does not remove all painful emotions. A wife may well forgive her husband for striking her in anger. But when she thinks about what he did, she may once again feel disappointment, hurt, and rejection. Forgiveness is not a feeling;

it is a commitment to accept the person in spite of what he or she has done. It is a decision not to demand justice but to show mercy.

Forgiveness does not remove the memory of the event. We speak of forgiving and forgetting. But ultimately, we never forget. Every event in life is recorded in the brain. There is every potential that the event will return to the conscious mind again and again. If we have chosen to forgive, we take the memory to God along with the hurt feelings, acknowledge to Him what we are thinking and feeling, but thank Him that by His grace the offense has been forgiven. Then we ask God for the power to do something kind and loving for that person today. We choose to focus on the future and not allow our minds to be obsessed with past failures that are now forgiven.

Assuming you are ready to express forgiveness, how might you verbalize it? Here are some suggestions.

STATEMENTS OF FORGIVENESS

I am deeply hurt by what you said. I think you realize that. I appreciate your apology, because without it, I don't think I could forgive you. But because I think you are sincere, I want you to know that I forgive you.

What can I say? I'm touched by your apology. I value our relationship greatly. Therefore, I'm choosing to forgive you.

I didn't know if I would ever be able to say this sincerely. I was devastated by what you did. I would never have imagined you capable of doing such a thing. But I love you, and I choose to believe that your apology is sincere. So I am offering you my forgiveness.

Your work error has cost me both time and money. I want to forgive you for causing this problem. Yes, I believe that with your correction plan in place, I can forgive you.

I know how hard it is for you to swallow your pride and say, "I was wrong." You've grown in my eyes, and I do forgive you.

TALK ABOUT IT

When do you find it most difficult to forgive someone? Why do you think this is the case?

Discuss the author's observation that "we are never separated from God's love, but our disobedience does separate us from His fellowship."

Why is it dangerous to forgive too easily?

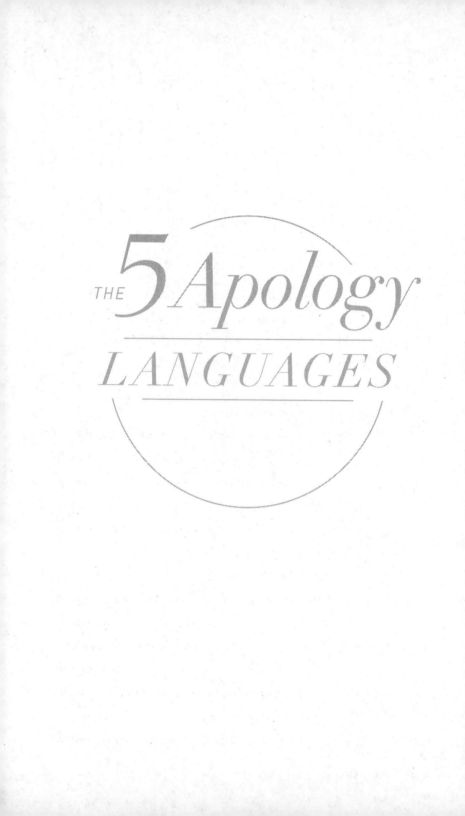

10

Healing Your Family Relationships

Kathleen shared a powerful testimony:

My parents were divorced when I was in fifth grade. When I would visit my dad, I didn't really feel like he cared about me or wanted to spend time with me. He remarried and divorced two more times and I stopped seeing him. Eventually my younger brother and I told our dad we didn't want anything to do with him. Then my younger brother committed suicide. I did not speak to my dad for five years.

During that time, he tried to contact me a few times, but always with the attitude of trying to explain why he was right and I was wrong. After a couple of years of silence—a time during which I started attending church and found a strong Christian friend—I decided I needed to forgive my dad and give him a second chance. So one day I picked up the phone and called him. That first call was short, but it was the beginning of a new relationship for my father and me.

That was over twenty years ago and I have maintained a healthy relationship with my father ever since. He now has Alzheimer's so our relationship has changed again, but I am grateful that I have had many good years with him!

The world is full of broken relationships between parents and children. Some, like Kathleen, are able to find a measure of healing and restoration. Others are not so fortunate.

Years ago when my son, Derek, was in graduate school, he lived and worked in a house church in the Haight-Ashbury district of San Francisco. His ministry focused on building relationships with young adults who had migrated to that city, hoping for a better life but found themselves homeless. At the end of three years in this ministry, Derek said to me, "Dad, almost every person I've gotten to know on the street is estranged from their parents. Most of them haven't had contact with family for years." I inquired about the kind of family dynamics that had led to such estrangement.

"Many of them were verbally, physically, or sexually abused by their parents," Derek answered. "As soon as they were old enough, they ran away and never looked back. However, others come out of homes that were fairly stable and supportive. But in the teenage years, they got involved in drugs. Their parents tried to help but eventually lost hope and gave up, leaving the young people to fend for themselves."

A Wayward Son

I once spent a week with Derek, walking the streets of San Francisco and meeting the people with whom he had built relationships. As I listened to the stories of these young adults, I wondered how many mothers and fathers in a distant city or in a rural town prayed daily that their child would return. I remembered the story that Jesus told about a young man who asked his father if he could have his inheritance while he was young rather than waiting until the death of his father. The father agreed, and the young man left with his pockets full of cash and a tidy sum in his savings account. The young man had followed the philosophy, "Eat, drink, and be merry, for tomorrow we die." In due time, he found himself penniless and took a job feeding pigs in order to sustain himself.[1]

One day he woke up with a memory of home and decided that he would travel home, apologize to his father, and ask if he could work as a hired employee on the family farm. Eventually, he turned his decision into reality and walked the long road back to his father, made his sincere apology, and expressed his desire to work as a hired hand on the farm. To his surprise, the father fully forgave and received him not as a hired hand but as a restored son.[2]

As I looked into the eyes of the young adults on the streets of San Francisco, I wondered how many of them might find reconciliation with parents if only the children would choose to apologize.

Children Who Are Willing to Apologize First

To be sure, those who were abused by parents needed also to receive an apology. But that was not likely to happen unless they initiated the process. Parents cannot apologize to an adult child with whom there is no contact. I remember the story of Marcie, whom I met at a marriage seminar in a Midwestern town. She had been sexually abused by her father; this had greatly affected her sexual relationship with her husband. At the urging of her husband, she went for counseling and soon gained insight into what had happened. Marcie decided to confront her father and deal with what had taken place so long ago. She knew that she did not cause the problem, but she also knew that for many years she had allowed bitterness and anger to keep her from seeking reconciliation with her parents. She had not seen them in many years.

With the help of her counselor and the support of her husband, Marcie called her parents and asked if she could come and see them. They agreed.

Marcie called it "the longest journey I've ever made and the most difficult conversation I've ever had. At the time I knew nothing about the five languages of apology," she said, "but I knew that I wanted to begin with an apology. In retrospect, I guess I tried to speak all five languages."

Marcie recalls what she said: "I've come to apologize for allowing anger, bitterness, and resentment to keep me away from you for all these years. I know that I was wrong to have done that. I am deeply sorry that we have lost all these years. I don't know if there is anything I can do to make that up to you, but I'm willing to try. I want the future to be different, and I've come to ask you if you will please forgive me."

By the end of her statement, both of her parents were crying. "My mother hugged me first, and then my father hugged me and said, 'Yes. Yes.' I was not prepared for what happened next. My father said, with tears in his eyes, 'I'll forgive you, but first I've got a lot of things that I need to ask you to forgive me for. I know that what I did to you was wrong. I've never discussed this with your mother, but I guess this is the time she needs to know that I abused you in an awful way. Since I've become a Christian, I've asked God to forgive me many times and I've shed many tears. And I hope that your mother can forgive me too.'

"I hugged my father and said, 'I do forgive you. I'm a Christian too, and I know that Christ died for your sins as well as mine.'

"My mother looked at my dad and said, 'I don't know if I can forgive you; to think that this is what kept my baby away from me all these years.'

"We spent the next two hours talking and crying together. I encouraged my parents to see a counselor so they could work through the emotions this had created. It was the beginning of a healing journey for all of us."

I must state clearly that, in my opinion, if her father had not apologized for his offense, the relationship would not have been restored. Marcie could not have apologized for her father; only he could do that. In her apology, she was dealing with her own failures; that is all any of us can do. But often, our willingness to apologize creates an emotional climate that makes it easier for the other person to apologize. I wondered how many of the young adults with whom I spoke on the streets of San Francisco might find a similar reunion if they chose to walk the road of apologizing.

APOLOGIZING TO YOUR ADULT CHILDREN

Now, let's look at the other side of the equation. There are no perfect parents. We have seen young adults accept their parents' apologies and genuinely forgive them for serious abuses. If you have an estranged relationship with your young adult child, why not take the initiative to apologize? Think of the years of pain that could have been avoided if Marcie's father had taken the initiative to confess his wrong and seek forgiveness years earlier. His embarrassment would have been a small price to pay for the emotional healing, and his asking forgiveness could have alleviated years of estrangement. Not all failures are as devastating as sexual abuse, but when we wrong our children, the results are always negative. Admitting our failures and asking our young adults to forgive us is the road to removing emotional barriers.

Recognize a Strained Relationship

Typically, the wrongs we have committed are not moral but rather relational. During one single adult conference, I spoke on the child/ parent relationship. Afterward, Sharon came to me and asked, "May I tell you my story?"

"Certainly," I said.

"My parents are good people," she began. "They have done much for me. In fact, that's the problem. They have done too much for me. I'm an only child, and they both devoted their lives to me. Their philosophy was 'Let me do it for you.' So I grew up with the feeling that I was not capable of doing anything. I remember that once when I was about seven, I made up my own bed that morning. My mother came in a few minutes later and said, 'Oh, my. What a mess,' and she proceeded to make up the bed her way. I guess she thought she was doing the right thing, but it fostered in me a spirit of inadequacy. I didn't do well in college, largely because of my self-concept."

"I love my parents very much," Sharon continued. "I think that their marriage was so insecure that they both found their only satisfaction in taking care of my needs. I wish they had taken care of each other and let me learn to take care of myself. I wish I could tell them what I feel, but I don't want to hurt them. Mom wonders why I don't come home more often."

I was extremely empathetic with Sharon. I have met many young adults who struggle with similar parental patterns. The parents are typically hardworking people who may have grown up with little. Their hard work has made them successful, and they want to do for their children what was not done for them. However, they do so much that their children never learn to do for themselves. Their "kindness" fosters a dependence that appears in several areas of life, the most obvious of which is financial. The young adult grows up knowing little about the value of money and feeling low motivation to work. Not only is the young adult financially handicapped, but he or she also has relational and emotional struggles.

If you are the parent of an adult child with whom you have a strained relationship or who in your opinion is underperforming in various areas of life, you may want to reflect upon your parenting patterns. It may be time for an apology.

Apologize Even When the Offense Is Unintended

It's not that you intentionally made mistakes. You were trying to care for your child. However, your behavior has made life more difficult for your son or daughter. Your apology cannot undo the emotional and relational inadequacies of your young adult, but it may well bring healing to your relationship. The fact that you are now seeing what the young adult has seen for many years but has been unwilling to share with you communicates to him or her that you are sensitive to your own failures and have the courage to admit them.

If you know the primary apology language of your young adult, be sure to include that in your apology. If you do not, then our suggestion is that you speak all five apology languages, and you are bound to hit it.

For example, if your young adult's primary apology language is *accepting responsibility*—i.e., what they want to hear is "I was wrong," and you leave this out of your apology—you may find that it does not have the desired results of reconciliation. A sincere apology opens up the possibility of forgiveness and true reconciliation.

APOLOGIZING TO BROTHERS AND SISTERS

Most siblings, in the process of growing up, do and say things that are hurtful to each other. If they were not taught to apologize, these hurts may become emotional barriers in their relationship. I remember Paul's visit to my counseling office. "I became a Christian about two years ago . . . but something really troubles me. My brother and I have a really bad relationship; in fact, I haven't spoken with him in five years. Since my mother's funeral, I haven't bothered to talk to him."

An Argument about a Tombstone

"So what happened to set this off?" I asked.

"Well, after the funeral my sister and I were talking with him about a tombstone for Mom's grave. He said he didn't believe in tombstones, that it was a waste of money. I got really angry with him and told him that if that was the way he felt, I didn't care to ever see him again. So my sister and I paid for the tombstone, and I haven't seen him since. It didn't bother me so much until I became a Christian, and I've been reading the Bible about forgiveness. And I think it is not right for me to hold that against him."

"What kind of relationship did you and your brother have before your mother's funeral?" I asked.

"We got along fairly well," he said. "I wouldn't say we were super close, but we never had any words with each other. We both respected each other. He didn't come to see Mom as much as I wished. I went by every day to see her; my sister saw her almost as often. But he came by maybe once a week. I guess the tombstone thing was just the straw that broke the camel's back."

"What about your father?" I inquired.

"He left us when we were all young. I haven't seen him in years.

Mom never remarried. She spent all of her energy working and trying to keep food on the table for us. I guess that's another reason I resent my brother's attitude."

"It's not hard for me to understand how that would upset you," I said. "I would probably be upset myself in that situation. But I think you would probably agree that you overreacted when you told him that you never wanted to see him again."

"I know," he said. "I was just so angry; that's the way I felt at the moment. But I know that I need to try to make it right. It's not right for brothers to live in the same town and not talk to each other."

"Have you ever heard your brother apologize to you for anything in the past?" I asked.

He thought for a moment and said, "I can't remember ever hearing him apologize to me. He did tell my sister that he was sorry that he didn't visit Mother more when she was sick. I was glad to hear that, but it was too late then."

I explained to Paul the languages of an apology and told him why I asked him if he had ever heard his brother apologize. "Typically, people speak the apology language they desire to receive," I explained. "Since he said to your sister that he was sorry that he didn't visit your mother more often when she was sick, I'm guessing that his apology language is *expressing regret*: 'I'm sorry. I feel bad about what I did.'"

"I've Really Missed You"

"Therefore, what I'm going to suggest is that you contact your brother and offer him an apology for the way you spoke to him and what you said to him about your mother's tombstone."

"That's going to be hard," he said.

"You are right. Probably one of the hardest things you've ever done in your life," I affirmed, "but perhaps one of the most productive." Together we worked on a possible apology statement. It looked something like this:

> I realize that I overreacted to you after Mom's funeral when we were talking about the tombstone. I feel bad about having said what I said to you. I know it was wrong, and I've thought a lot about it since then. I really am sorry that I said that. I don't know if you can forgive me, but I would like to ask you to forgive me. If there is anything I can do to make it up to you, I'd like to do it. I just feel bad that I've treated you that way and told you that I didn't want to see you again. I've really missed you. I know I can't take back the words, but I do want to say that I am sorry that I ever said those words. That's not really what I desire, and I hope that you can forgive me.

Paul read the apology aloud, and tears came to his eyes. "That's really the way I feel," he said. "I'd like an opportunity to say this to him. How do I go about it?" he asked.

"I suggest you call him on the phone and ask him if you could come by and see him for a few minutes one evening. If he says no, then I suggest you wait a month and call him again. But I have an idea that he may say yes. If so, when you arrive at his house, don't spend a lot of time in small talk. Get right to the point and let him know that you've come to apologize to him for something that has been bothering you for a long time. After you've seen your brother, I'd like for you to give me a call, because I'd like to know how it went." He agreed and thanked me for our time together.

His Brother's Response

Six weeks later, I got a call from Paul, asking for a follow-up appointment.

"Great. I'd like to hear it."

A couple of days later Paul came to my office. "I can't tell you how glad I am that I took your advice," he said. "It was one of the most difficult things I've ever done in my life, but when I apologized to my brother, he started crying. He said, 'I know what I said was wrong. I should have helped pay for Mom's tombstone. I don't know; I've never been much for sentimental things. But I know it was wrong. At first, I was hurt and angry with your response. But later I realized that you had a right to say what you said. I probably would have said the same thing if I had been in your shoes. So I guess what I'm saying is I will forgive you if you will forgive me.'

"We hugged each other, and both of us cried for a long time. And then my brother said, 'I want you to tell me how much the tombstone cost, because I want to pay you and Sis for my part.'

"'You don't need to do that,' I said. 'Just the fact that we've gotten back together is enough payment for me.'

"'I know, but I want to do it for my sake and for Mom,' he said with tears running down his face.

"'Okay,' I said. 'I'll try to find the papers and let you know how much it was.' Then we sat down and talked for an hour about what had been going on in our lives since Mom died. It was a wonderful time, and I feel like our relationship has been restored. We're having him and his wife over to our house next week for a cookout. My wife and I are excited to learn what's been going on in their lives. Thanks for giving me the courage to apologize," he said.

"I'm glad you followed through," I said. "Few things are more powerful in human relationships than learning to accept responsibility for failures and to sincerely apologize to the person we have wronged."

I believe that many sibling relationships could be healed if someone was willing to take the initiative and apologize. I cannot guarantee that all apologies will be as successful in restoring relationships as was Paul's apology, but I can assure you that relationships are always better when someone chooses to apologize.

APOLOGIZING TO YOUR IN-LAWS

No matter how much we may be devoted to our in-laws, these relationships can be difficult to navigate for one basic reason: marriage brings together two sets of traditions and patterns of family relationships. These differences almost inevitably create conflicts. Failure to deal with these conflicts can create years of "in-law problems."

I remember the couple who sat in my office some months ago. "We don't understand our daughter-in-law," said Katherine. "She has told us that she doesn't want us to visit our grandchildren without calling or texting and making sure it is convenient for her. What kind of relationship is that?"

Her husband, Curtis, added: "I grew up in a home where my grandparents stopped by almost every day. It was one of the highlights of my childhood. We like our daughter-in-law. When she was dating Alan, we were pleased when they announced that they were going to get married. But it's like now that they have children, she's changed. Why would she want to make everything so difficult?"

"Probably because she's a wife and mother and employee and a choir member," I said. "And life gets pretty hectic; for you to drop by unexpectedly is another stress factor for her."

I could tell they were shocked at my answer, so I continued talking.

"Do she and Alan often ask you to babysit with the children?" I asked.

"Almost every week," Katherine said. "That's the thing about it. We try to help them out so they can have time together, and then she treats us this way."

I tried to explain to them the difference in family dynamics and the difference in generational patterns. "When you were children, life was much simpler, easier, and slower; and neighbors often visited with neighbors. Now it's screens, swimming classes, dance classes, piano lessons, Little League, etc. Family life is much busier. For the average family, there is very little leisure time. Consequently, to have in-laws visit whenever it is convenient for them often puts greater stress on the young couple as they seek to rear their children."

I told them that their daughter-in-law's request that they call or text before coming and make sure it was convenient for them was not abnormal in today's culture. I suggested that Katherine and Curtis make the most of the opportunities they get to babysit with their grandchildren and recognize those times as their primary opportunities for interacting with them.

Then I suggested that they needed to apologize to their daughter-in-law for being insensitive to the stress their unannounced visits were causing. I could tell that this was not the way they had expected this conversation to end. But I could also tell that they were grappling with what I was saying and trying to understand. I commended them for coming to see me and trying to get help rather than letting this simply continue until they ended up doing or saying something very destructive to the in-law relationship.

"You are at a very crucial point in your relationship with your daughter-in-law," I suggested. "I think that a sincere apology from you will mend the hurt and allow you to have a positive relationship in the future. Do you know your daughter-in-law's primary apology language?" I asked. The blank look in their eyes told me that was a new concept. So I explained to them the five languages of apology and why it was important to speak the other person's primary apology language.

"I think her language must be accepting responsibility," Katherine said, "because Alan told us that when they have spats, she wants him to say, 'I was wrong,' and that anything short of that she doesn't consider an apology."

"Then let's assume that is her primary apology language," I said, "so be sure you include that in your apology. It won't hurt to throw in some of the other languages as well." We spent the next few minutes working on a possible apology statement. Here's what we ended up with:

> We have realized that our coming by unannounced has put unnecessary pressure on you and Alan and the children. That is certainly not our desire. We realize that has been wrong, and we would like to ask you to forgive us. In both our childhoods, life was a lot different; much slower and people stopped by all the time unannounced. But we know that it's different now. We all live with a lot of pressure. You have work and church and all the kids' activities. We certainly want to respect that. We appreciate your letting us babysit the children. We enjoy those times. So feel free to call on us anytime. And we promise we will try not to just stop by but always call to see if it is convenient. And if not, we won't take it personally, because we know how stressful life can be sometimes. We love you two so much, and we want you to have good family relationships and a strong marriage. We want to be an asset and not a liability. So will you forgive us for being a little pushy in the past? We know it was wrong, and we want to make it different in the future.

Later they told me that their apology was successful and they felt that their relationship with their daughter-in-law was now healthy. "I guess we've got to learn to live in the twenty-first century," they said. "Thanks for helping us."

Most troubled in-law relationships could be mended if someone were willing to apologize and learn how to express the apology in the language of the other person.

The same is true with every other family relationship: grandparents and grandchildren, aunts and uncles and cousins, and certainly within stepfamilies. But whether you're part of a large, close-knit clan all living in the same town, or your extended family is spread around the country or around the world and you keep in touch by Zoom and social media, learning to give and receive apologies will go a long way toward healing your family relationships.

TALK ABOUT IT

Have you ever experienced or observed a broken or damaged relationship in your family?

"Most siblings, in the process of growing up, do and say things that are hurtful to each other." How have you dealt with that in your own life?

In what ways can writing an apology statement help in dealing with an emotional issue? Can you think of a time when writing out your apology would have better helped the situation?

THE 5 Apology
LANGUAGES

11

Choosing to Forgive Yourself

Jordan had always been the all-American model teenager. Good
student, star soccer player, active in the church youth program—
but now he was sitting in my office in tears. I have known him all his
life, but I had never seen him this distraught.

He spoke slowly at first, trying to hold back the tears.

"I've really blown it," he said. "I've messed up my whole life. I
really wish I could die."

"Would you like to tell me about it?" I asked. Jordan looked at the
floor as he talked.

"It all started last year," he said. "I met this girl at school. I knew I
shouldn't have dated her, but she was so good-looking. I started taking her home after school. I found out her father had left four years
ago and her mother didn't get home from work until about 6:00 p.m.
We would study together and talk. Then we started messing around,
and before long, we were having sex. I knew it wasn't right, but I

tried to be careful. She got pregnant anyway, and last week she had an abortion."

Jordan's whole body was shaking. Tears were falling on his jeans like rain. A full minute later, he said, "I let my parents down. I let God down. I let myself down. I let her down. I just wish I could die."

Jordan was young, but he was wise enough to know that he needed help. For the next twelve months, I saw him regularly. I watched him step up to the plate and apologize to his parents, the young woman, and her mother. I saw him weep as he acknowledged to God that he had sinned and asked for His forgiveness. Near the end of our year of counseling (he was now a freshman in college), Jordan said to me, "I think there is one more apology I need to make."

"What's that?" I asked.

"I think I need to apologize to myself."

"That's interesting. Why would you say that?"

"I keep beating myself up," he said. "I keep remembering what I did and feeling bad about it. I don't think I have ever forgiven myself. Everybody else seems to have forgiven me—but *I* haven't forgiven me. Maybe if I could apologize to myself, I could forgive myself."

"I think you're dead right," I said. "Why don't we work on an apology? What would you like to say to yourself?"

Jordan started talking and I started writing. "I'd like to tell myself that I did wrong; I mean really wrong, grossly wrong. I'd like to tell myself how bad I feel about it and how much I regret what I did. I'd like to tell myself that I have learned my lesson, and I will keep myself sexually pure from now until the day I get married. I'd like to give myself the freedom to be happy again. And I'd like to ask myself to forgive me and to help me make the most of my life in the future."

I had been writing furiously to capture Jordan's words. "Give me just a moment," I said. I turned to my computer and typed in Jordan's apology, inserting his name. I printed off a copy and turned to him and said, "I want you to stand in front of this mirror and give your apology to yourself." I listened and watched as Jordan read his apology. Here is what Jordan said:

Jordan, I want to tell you that I did wrong; I mean really wrong, grossly wrong. Jordan, I want to tell you how bad I feel about it and how much I regret what I did. I want to tell you that I have learned my lesson, and I will keep myself sexually pure from now until the day I get married. I want to give myself the freedom to be happy again. And, Jordan, I want to ask you to forgive me and to help me make the most of my life in the future.

Then Jordan turned to me, and I said, "Go ahead, read the last sentence." He continued, *"Jordan, because I believe your apology is sincere, I choose to forgive you."*

The tears were flowing freely down his face as he turned and we embraced. For a full minute we both wept in the thrill of forgiveness. Jordan went on to finish college and is now married, with his own family. He said to me several years after our counseling experience, "The most significant part of my journey was the day I apologized and forgave myself. I don't think I would have made it if that had not happened."

As a counselor, I learned from Jordan firsthand the tremendous power of apologizing to oneself.

WHO WE ARE—WHO WE WANT TO BE

Why would you apologize to yourself? In a general sense, you apologize to yourself for the same reason you apologize to someone else: you want to restore the relationship. When you apologize to someone else, you hope the apology will remove the barrier between the two of you so that your relationship can continue to grow. When you apologize to yourself, you are seeking to remove the emotional disequilibrium between the person you *want* to be (the ideal self) and the person you *are* (the real self). The greater the distance between the ideal self and the real self, the greater the intensity of the inner emotional turmoil. Being "at peace with oneself" occurs when we remove the distance between the ideal self and the real self. Apologizing to oneself—and subsequently experiencing forgiveness—serves to remove the distance.

Sometimes the emotional anxiety stems from failure to live up to one's moral standards. This was the case with Jordan. He had promised himself that he would never become sexually active before marriage. He knew this was not a moral standard accepted by all teenagers but for him it was a spiritual issue. He believed that this was God's standard, and he intended to follow it. When he consciously violated his moral standards, he was assailed by anxiety and guilt. For him, the distance between the ideal self and the real self was immense. His apologies to others had served to heal relationships, but until he apologized to himself, he did not find inner peace.

Moral failures occur on many fronts. Neal was a forty-five-year-old father of two. He had taught his boys from an early age to tell the truth. Integrity was a high moral value for him, and he wanted his boys to learn to tell the truth. One year as he was filling out his federal tax return, he "stretched the truth" in order to get a larger deduction.

At the time, it seemed like a little thing and inconsequential. But within a week, Neal was experiencing strong misgivings about what he had done. It was not until he filed an amended tax return and apologized and forgave himself that he felt better.

Lying, stealing, cheating, and sexual immorality are all examples of broken moral standards that can lead to guilt and anxiety. While apologizing to others may bring healing to human relationships, self-apology and forgiveness remove the anxiety and restore peace of mind.

Not all bad behavior is immoral or even very significant. Still, when we feel we've behaved badly, our view of ourselves is damaged. We thought we were "more mature"—and we beat ourselves up.

Ellen from New England said to me, "I can't believe I was so immature. I created a scene over a discrepancy in a meal charge. I treated the waiter harshly and drew attention to myself from people at other tables. I have been reliving that scene for weeks now. I used to think I was a pretty decent person . . . but now I don't know."

Ellen is suffering with damaged self-esteem. The difference between her ideal self and real self are causing her great emotional pain. Ellen needs to apologize to herself.

Then there's Davis, an aspiring businessman who made an unwise response to another businessman in town. He said to me, "I feel like I shot myself in the foot. I apologized to the person involved, and I think he's forgiven me. But I am afraid that what I did is going to affect my business for a long time to come. I'm having a hard time shaking it and getting motivated to go on. I've even thought about moving to another city and starting over." Davis is struggling with intense anxiety over the matter, and it is affecting the way he operates his business. He needs to apologize to himself so he can focus on the future and not on past failures.

When you are plagued with anxiety over a past failure, the answer is not "trying to forget it." The more you try to forget it, the bigger it becomes in your mind. The answer lies in apologizing to the offended parties and then apologizing and forgiving yourself.

WHEN YOU'RE ANGRY AT YOURSELF

When we fail to live up to our ideal self, what happens inside of us is what happens inside others when we offend them: we become angry. This anger is turned toward self and is often expressed through *implosion* or *explosion*.

When we explode with anger, we damage our relationships with others. When we implode, we damage ourselves. This may take the form of berating yourself mentally. *I'm stupid; I'm dumb; I'll never get it right; I'll never amount to anything. What's wrong with me?* These are the attitudes of implosive anger. An extreme case of implosion may express itself by physically abusing one's body. Wrist cutting, head banging, and starvation are examples of personal physical abuse. Self-anger expressed by explosion or implosion never improves a situation.

Anger at yourself when you feel you've "blown it" in some way is normal. But here is the healthy way to process that anger. First, admit to yourself that what you did was unwise, wrong, or hurtful to others and to yourself. Second, apologize to the people you have offended, and hope they will forgive you. Third, consciously apologize to yourself and choose to forgive yourself.

HOW DO I APOLOGIZE TO MYSELF?

Apologizing to oneself requires *self-talk*. Perhaps you have heard someone say, "Talking to yourself is a sign of mental illness." Wrong! Mentally healthy people always talk to themselves—encouraging themselves, advising themselves, questioning themselves. Some of this self-talk is done aloud; much of it is done inwardly and silently. One woman I know said, "When I have a tough challenge ahead of me, I will always murmur aloud, over and over, '*You can do this.*' It helps!"

And when it comes to apologizing to yourself, I like to encourage audible self-talk. If you are aware of your own apology language, then focus on speaking that language, but include the other four languages for additional emotional credit.

At the time I counseled with Jordan, I had not discovered the five languages of an apology. However, in retrospect Jordan did an excellent job of speaking all five languages to himself. My guess is that Jordan's primary apology language was accepting responsibility. I say that because he began his self-apology by saying, "I did wrong; really and grossly wrong. I really regret what I did." I have discovered that when people offer an apology, many times they will begin by expressing it in their own apology language. They are saying to others what they would expect others to say to them if they were apologizing.

We suggest that you write out your self-apology before you speak it to yourself. Here is a summary of the apology that Jordan made to himself. We have removed his name and left the blanks so you can include your name. You may change the order of his statements, and you may change the wording. We offer it simply to help you get started in forming your self-apology.

"_____, I want to tell you that I did wrong; I mean really wrong, grossly wrong. _____, I want to tell you how bad I feel about it and how much I regret what I did. I want to tell you that I have learned my lesson. _____, I want to give myself the freedom to be happy again. And, _____, I want to ask you to forgive me and to help me make the most of my life in the future. _____, because I believe your apology is sincere, I choose to forgive you."

Go ahead and write your self-apology statement. After you have written that self-apology, we encourage you to stand in front of the mirror, look yourself in the eyes, and audibly offer your apology to yourself. We believe that apologizing to yourself is an important step in the process of restoring "peace with yourself."

WHAT DOES IT MEAN TO FORGIVE MYSELF?

Forgiving oneself is much like forgiving someone who has offended you. Forgiving someone else means that you choose to no longer hold the offense against them. You will accept them back into your life and will seek to continue building your relationship with them. Their offense is no longer a barrier in your relationship. If a wall is seen as a symbol of their offense against you, forgiveness tears down the wall. Forgiveness allows the two of you to communicate again and to listen to each other with a view to understanding. It opens up the potential of working together as a team.

The same is true in forgiving oneself. At its root, self-forgiveness is a choice. We feel pained at our wrongdoing. We wish we had not committed the offense. The reality is that we have. We have apologized to other parties who were involved if our offense was against others. Perhaps we have asked God's forgiveness. We have also apologized to ourselves. Now it is time to forgive ourselves. We must choose to do so. No positive purpose is served by berating ourselves explosively or implosively. All such behavior is destructive. Choosing to forgive oneself removes the distance between the ideal self and the real self. In forgiving ourselves, we are affirming our high ideals. We are admitting our failures and affirming our commitment to our ideals.

As you wrote your self-apology statement, we also encourage you to write your self-forgiveness statement. Here is a sample that may stimulate your own thinking.

"_____, the offense you committed has troubled me greatly. It has brought me much inner anxiety. But I have heard your sincere apology and I value you. Therefore, _____, I choose to forgive you. I will no longer hold the offense against you. I will do everything I can to make your future bright. You can count on my support. Let me say it again, _____: I forgive you."

After you have written your forgiveness statement, again we urge you to stand in front of the mirror, look yourself in the eyes, and audibly express your forgiveness.

As in forgiving others, this self-forgiveness does not remove all the pain or memories of your failure, nor does it necessarily remove all the results of your failure. For example, if you have lied or stolen, you may still face the results of those actions. What forgiveness does is release you from the bondage of your past failures and give you the freedom to make the most of the future.

LEARNING FROM YOUR FAILURES

You are now in a position to change the course of your life. Sometimes people make the mistake of trying never to think again about the failure. The fact is we can learn much from our failures. Ask yourself, *What are the factors that led me to the offense?* Those are things that need to be changed.

For example, if you fell into the abuse of alcohol or drugs, it may be that you put yourself into a situation that fostered drinking or drug use. In the future, you must not allow this to happen. If your failure was sexual immorality, then you must remove yourself from the environment that would encourage you to repeat that failure.

In addition to learning from past failures, you are now in a position to take positive steps to make your future brighter. This may involve reading books, attending seminars, talking with friends, or counseling. These are the kinds of steps that give you new information and insights with which to direct your future. Apologizing to yourself and choosing to forgive yourself opens to you the possibility of a future that is far brighter than you have ever dreamed.

TALK ABOUT IT

Why does it seem easier at times to forgive other people than to forgive ourselves? How have you seen this in your life?

Share an experience you have had in taking "positive steps" to overcome a challenge.

What do you think of the idea of talking with yourself about self-apology? Does it feel natural or awkward? How has your background influenced how you view this concept of self-talk?

THE 5 Apology LANGUAGES

12

Truly Sorry, Truly Forgiven

S teven Spielberg's award-winning movie *Lincoln* looks at the
months in the great president's life when he was pushing for
passage of the Emancipation Proclamation. The success of the film,
as well as the racial reckoning that Americans have wrestled with
in recent years, has reminded Americans once again of our sorrow-
ful history of enslavement of and violence toward Black citizens.
Much has been said over the years about "apologizing" for enslavement, about making reparations and effecting reconciliation. The
same has happened in regard to other unjustly treated groups such
as Japanese-Americans who were interned during World War II,
Chinese immigrants who faced tremendous discrimination in the
nineteenth century, or Native Americans who suffered so greatly as
our nation expanded westward.

And today, when so many conflicts are "resolved" at the point of a
gun, we must ask: What would happen if we all learned to apologize

168 • THE 5 APOLOGY LANGUAGES

more effectively? If we learned to forgive and accept forgiveness?

These national conversations are ongoing, challenging, and absolutely necessary. And, sometimes, learning to forgive happens much closer to home.

WHAT WE ALL NEED

When our granddaughter Davy Grace was five, her mother and father allowed her to spend a special week with Grandma and Grandpa. Karolyn and I were elated. The week was great fun. But one experience is indelibly printed in my memory. Karolyn has a special drawer where she keeps "stickers" for the grandchildren. Davy Grace, of course, knew about this special drawer and asked her grandmother if she could have some stickers. Karolyn told her that she could have three, any three she chose.

An hour or two later, we began to see stickers all over the house. Davy Grace had taken the entire sheet of stickers and placed them randomly. Karolyn said to her, "I thought I told you to take only three stickers, but you have taken the whole sheet."

Davy Grace stood in silence as her grandmother continued. "You disobeyed Grandmother."

Tears cascaded down Davy Grace's face as she said, "I need somebody to forgive me."

I shall never forget those words nor the pain that I saw in her young face. My tears joined her tears as I embraced her and said, "Honey, all of us need somebody to forgive us. And Papa will be happy to forgive you, and I'm sure Grandmother will also." Karolyn joined us in our hug of reconciliation.

SOMEBODY TO FORGIVE US

I have reflected upon that scene many times while I have been writing this book on apology. I'm convinced that the need for forgiveness is universal and that acknowledging that need is the essence of an apology.

Apologies grow out of an awareness that my words or behavior has violated the trust of others or has offended them in some way. When these offenses go unacknowledged, the relationship is fractured. I live with a sense of guilt or a smug self-righteousness while the offended party lives with hurt, disappointment, and/or anger. We both know that our relationship has suffered from the offense. If neither of us extends the olive branch, the quality of our relationship will continue to diminish.

Years ago while living in Chicago, I often volunteered at the Pacific Garden Mission. I met scores of men and a few women who shared with me their journey to the streets. I recognized a common thread through all of their stories. All of them had a series of experiences in which someone treated them unfairly—at least this was their perception. And no one ever apologized. Many of them admitted that they also had treated others unkindly and failed to apologize. A string of broken relationships was the result. Eventually, there was no one to whom they could turn, so they turned to the streets. I have often wondered how different things might have been had someone taught these men and women to apologize.

On the other end of the social spectrum is corporate America. In recent years, we have seen numerous corporate executives indicted and sometimes convicted of fraud. One wonders what would have happened if these executives had learned to apologize when they were climbing up the corporate ladder.

Many government employees have also joined the ranks of the convicted. Most of them have pleaded innocent until they were proven guilty. When apologies have been made, they tended to be stated in very nebulous terms and often appeared self-serving. In the case of government and public executives, the reluctance to apologize may grow out of fear that the apology will be used against them. They reason, *Better to keep quiet and maintain my position than to apologize and lose everything.* Many have never come to understand that there are things in life more important than power and money. Albert Einstein once wrote, "Sometimes what counts can't be counted, and what can be counted doesn't count."[1]

Breaking the Patterns of Our Culture

For the "ordinary" man or woman, the reluctance to apologize is rooted in cultural patterns that they observed and internalized while growing up. Thus, as we have discussed earlier, some jump immediately into the blame mode, blaming others for their failures. Others, with a stone face, deny that any offense has been committed. Still others make a quick and weak apology, hoping to put the matter behind them.

However, a growing number of people are learning to slow down and take time to genuinely apologize. These are the strong ones; these are the heroes; these are the ones whom people like to be around; these are the ones whom people trust.

IF APOLOGIES WERE A WAY OF LIFE . . .

The art of apologizing is not easy, but it can be learned, and it is worth the effort. Apologizing opens up a whole new world of emotional and spiritual health. Having apologized, we are able to look ourselves in the mirror, look people in the eyes, and worship God "in spirit and in truth." It is those who truly apologize who are most likely to be truly forgiven.

If apologizing were a way of life, no walls would be built. Relationships would be authentic. Certainly people would fail, but the failures would be dealt with in an open and honest manner. Regret would be expressed; responsibility would be accepted. Restitution would be made. Planned change or changes would be our intention, and we would stand humbly and say, "I need somebody to forgive me." I believe in most cases if we learned to apologize effectively, we would be genuinely forgiven.

When apology becomes a way of life, relationships will remain healthy. People will find the acceptance, support, and encouragement they need. Fewer people would turn to drugs and alcohol in an effort to find escape from broken relationships. And fewer people would live on the streets of America.

Yes, Davy Grace, I too need somebody to forgive me. From five to eighty-five, we all need someone to forgive us. That is more likely to happen if we learn to apologize effectively. May this book move all of us into the apology mode. May we learn to recognize and overcome our tendency to blame, deny, or offer quick and weak apologies without truly dealing with the offense.

As we close this book, perhaps you would like to join us in this prayer: "Father, give me the attitude of Davy Grace: 'I need somebody to forgive me,' and teach me how to apologize effectively. Amen."

TALK ABOUT IT

Take some time to discuss some of the conflicts and ills in our society. How would "admitting wrong" help heal some of these ills?

THINGS *NOT* TO SAY WHEN APOLOGIZING

When do you tune out of an apology and decide the other person is insincere? Often, we reject an apology as soon as we hear words that blame, excuse, or deny. Do you want to use best practices for apologies that actually work? If so, omit these phrases. When I am sitting in my counselor chair and I hear these phrases being spoken to a partner, I often stop the action and say, "You are heading in the WRONG direction. Proceed only if you intend to wreck this relationship."

- Haven't you gotten over that yet?
- I am sorry that you were offended.
- I asked for and received forgiveness from God.
- I should be excused because I . . .
- You're too sensitive. I was only joking.
- Why do you always . . . ?
- If you hadn't . . .
- You sound like your mother.
- That's just silly.
- That's life.
- What's the big deal?
- To the extent that you were offended . . .
- Give me a break.
- You just need to get over it.
- There is nothing I can do about that now. I can't take away the past!
- Why can't you let bygones be bygones?

THINGS *TO* SAY WHEN APOLOGIZING

What is the right way to apologize? There are two good methods: you could write down the apology and then read it to the person, or you could just say it. Do not try to give a serious apology via electronic media. Taking the time to speak directly with someone better conveys your sincerity.

What are the steps for giving a good apology? Body language can make or break the sincerity of an apology. Be sure that you maintain eye contact, don't cross your arms defensively, listen with concern, and speak with a pleasant tone of voice. Then, choose words that do not blame others, excuse yourself, or deny responsibility. Instead, take responsibility for your part of the problem (do this even if it wasn't all your fault), express sorrow for hurt feelings, offer to make amends, talk about how you can prevent the problem from happening again, and consider requesting forgiveness.

Here is a useful phrase to help you jump back into an issue: "I'd like to circle back to (name the issue). I realize that I didn't say (or do) things the right way. I apologize for that." This method brings you back to the topic and it shows your intent to be open and nondefensive.

Next, use some of these tried and true apology phrases. Use more than one of these if they really apply to your situation, if the offense has happened repeatedly, and/or if the damage was serious:

- I did it, and I have no excuse.
- I'm responsible for the mistake.
- It might take us a long time to move on from what I've done.
- I would have a hard time forgiving me if I were you.

- I've damaged your trust.

- I was careless, insensitive, thoughtless, or rude.

- I will do the work to fix my mistake going forward.

- My actions were unacceptable.

- My heart aches over what I've done.

- You didn't deserve that kind of treatment.

- You have every right to be upset.

- I know that what I did was wrong.

- My mistake is part of a pattern that I need to change.

- I will rebuild your trust by . . .

- I will try to make this up to you by . . .

- I've put you in a very difficult position.

- I realize that talk is cheap. I know that I need to show you how I will change.

- I hope I haven't waited too long to give you the apology you deserve.

- Can you ever forgive me?

THE 5 Apology
LANGUAGES

The Apology Language Profile

The following profile is designed to help you discover your primary apology language.

To Get Started: Think of a time that you've dealt with an offense at home or in your workplace and you wanted to mend the relationship. Hold that experience in your head as you consider the following twenty-five paired statements. Please circle the letter next to the statement that best defines what is most meaningful to you in apologies from others. Both statements may (or may not) sound like they fit your situation, but please choose the statement that captures the essence of what is most meaningful to you, the majority of the time. Allow ten to fifteen minutes to complete the profile. Take it when you are relaxed, and try not to rush through it.

1. *It's more meaningful to me when I hear someone say . . .*

    A "I deeply regret having embarrassed you like I did."

    E "Our friendship really is important to me. Will you please forgive me?"

2. *It's more meaningful to me when someone says . . .*

    B "OK, I admit it—I made a big mistake."

    D "I want to grow from this experience. Would you be willing to help me figure out steps to handle this type of situation better?"

3. *It's more meaningful to me when someone tells me . . .*

    C "What can I do or say to make things right between you and me?"

    B "I had a bad attitude and it showed. I should have thought more about what I was doing."

4. *It's more meaningful to me when someone says . . .*

    D "I don't want to do this again. So I will come up with ways to avoid mistakes like this in the future."

    E "I apologize for my actions. You obviously don't have to forgive me, but I hope you will."

5. *It's more meaningful to me when someone asks me . . .*

    E "Can you possibly forgive me?"

    C "What can I do to mend our relationship?"

6. *It's more meaningful to me when I hear someone say . . .*

    B "I totally messed up. I could make excuses, but really, I have no good excuse for my actions."

E   "You have every right to hold this against me, but will you please consider forgiving me?"

7. *It's more meaningful to me when someone asks me . . .*

C   "I'd like to make things better between us. What can I do to make things right?"

E   "You don't have to answer immediately, but will you consider forgiving me for making this mistake?"

8. *It's more meaningful to me when I hear these words from someone . . .*

E   "I want to ask you to forgive to me."

A   "It deeply pains me to see you hurting like this."

9. *It's more meaningful to me when someone says . . .*

B   "I've really messed up this time. We missed the deadline because of me."

C   "Can we back up and let me try to fix this? I really want to mend the damage I've caused."

10. *It's more meaningful to me when I hear someone say . . .*

A   "I am upset with myself over how I handled our disagreement. I cringe when I recall the way I acted."

D   "I know that what I've been doing is not helpful. What would you like to see me change that would make this better for you?"

11. *It's more meaningful to me when someone tells me . . .*

B   "I know that what I did was wrong."

A   "I'm so sorry—I feel terrible that I let you down."

12. *It's more meaningful to me when someone asks me . . .*

    D   "What changes could I put into place so that you might begin to trust me going forward?"

    E   "I hope this won't permanently damage our working relationship. Will you please accept my apology?"

13. *It's more meaningful to me when someone says . . .*

    A   "I can see my actions caused you pain, and I feel terrible about what I did."

    C   "Is there anything I can do to repair the damage I've created?"

14. *It's more meaningful to me when someone tells me . . .*

    B   "If I had only thought about what I was doing, I would have realized it was wrong."

    E   "I know that I've caused you a significant amount of trouble. I would greatly appreciate it if you would forgive me."

15. *It's more meaningful to me when I hear someone say . . .*

    A   "I am truly grieved and sorry for my actions and the ways they affected you."

    D   "If I am ever again upset with you, I promise to gather my thoughts and approach you directly and respectfully."

16. *It's more meaningful to me when someone says . . .*

    E   "I hope that you can find it in your heart to forgive me."

    B   "I simply should not have done that."

17. *It's more meaningful to me when I hear someone say . . .*

    D   "I realize that talk is cheap. I'll work to show you that I'm changing."

    C   "Is there anything I can do to make up for what I did?"

18. *It's more meaningful to me when someone tells me . . .*

   A   "I really am embarrassed about my behavior—and I'm so, so sorry."

   B   "No ifs, ands or buts. I admit that I was wrong."

19. *It's more meaningful to me when I hear someone say . . .*

   E   "I apologize. Will you please forgive me?"

   D   "Going forward, I will manage my time and prioritize my schedule so that I won't have the same difficulties."

20. *It's more meaningful to me when someone says . . .*

   D   "I want so badly to avoid this type of error again. Let's talk about what I can do in the future to follow through on my commitments."

   C   "I don't feel right just saying 'my bad.' I want to make up for what I've done. What would you consider appropriate?"

21. *It's more meaningful to me when someone tells me . . .*

   B   "I know that my actions were totally unacceptable. I own that."

   A   "It stresses me out to know that you had to stand there waiting on me. I regret the frustration and worry that I caused you."

22. *It's more meaningful to me when someone says . . .*

   C   "I know that I've inconvenienced you. What can I do for you that could help balance things out?"

   A   "I am unhappy with how I've hurt you—I'm enormously disappointed in myself."

23. *It's more meaningful to me when I hear these words from someone . . .*

C "What can I do to make this situation right for you—immediately?"

D "It may take some time to rebuild your trust in me—meanwhile, I'm working hard on changes to prove that I am trustworthy."

24. *It's more meaningful to me when someone says . . .*

A "I am so sorry about that. I feel truly awful about having disappointed you."

C "Saying 'I'm sorry' doesn't feel like it is enough. What more can I say or do to make this up to you?"

25. *It's more meaningful to me when someone says . . .*

D "I'm confident that everything I've learned from this bad experience will prevent me from doing it again."

B "I know what I did was inappropriate—no two ways about it."

Now go back and count the number of times you circled each individual letter and write that number in the appropriate blank below.

RESULTS

_____ A: Express Regret

_____ B: Accept Responsibility

_____ C: Make Restitution

_____ D: Planned Change

_____ E: Request Forgiveness

Which apology language received the highest score? This is your primary apology language. If point totals for two apology languages are equal, you are "bilingual" and have two primary apology languages. And, if you have a secondary apology language, or one that is close in score to your primary apology language, this means that both expressions of apology are important to you. The highest possible score for any single apology language is 10.

Knowing the apology languages is powerful, but knowing how they work in your relationships—that is a real game changer.

LEARN MORE AT

www.apologylanguages.com and www.5LoveLanguages.com

THE 5 Apology LANGUAGES

Acknowledgments

We would need to apologize if we did not acknowledge our appreciation for the hundreds of couples who took time to complete our apology questionnaire and for the scores who gave us extensive interviews. Without their help, this book could not have been written. Many of these couples spoke honestly of their own failures at apologizing and forgiving. Others shared the journey that led them to discovering the art of apologizing effectively and finding the joy of reconciliation. The book is enriched by the honesty of these couples.

Both of us are also indebted to the couples and individuals who have turned to us for counsel. Many of the clients who have sat in our offices have been there because someone failed to apologize. Their stories have taught us the pain of rejection and, in some cases, the joy of seeing them learn how to give and receive an apology and thus open the door to forgiveness and reconciliation. We have changed their names and certain details to protect their privacy, but their stories add much to this book.

A special thanks to Tricia Kube, who computerized the manuscript and gave us great encouragement; to Shannon Warden, who created the "Apology Profile" found at the end of the book and who also was a great help in collecting and organizing our research questionnaires; and to Kay Tatum, our technical guru who made the manuscript presentable for the publisher. Also, a special thanks to Rob Eagar of WildFire Marketing for his skilled coaching.

We are also grateful to Greg Thornton, John Hinkley, Betsey Newenhuyse, and the wonderful team at Moody Publishers. Not only did they do a superb job of editing and positioning the book, they also gave us much encouragement as we did our research and writing.

Finally, we each want to thank our spouses, Karolyn and J.T., to whom we dedicate this volume. Without their love and support, neither of us would have had the emotional energy to complete the project. This book is a tribute to their generous spirits.

—GARY CHAPMAN, PhD
—JENNIFER THOMAS, PhD

Notes

Chapter 1: Righting Wrongs
1. Matthew 6:15 NKJV.
2. Ephesians 4:32; 1 John 1:9.
3. Luke 23:34.
4. Acts 2:22–24, 40–41.
5. Romans 12:19.
6. For a further explanation of how to release stored anger, see Gary Chapman, *Anger: Handling a Powerful Emotion in a Healthy Way* (Chicago: Northfield, 2007).
7. Dietrich Bonhoeffer, *The Cost of Discipleship* (New York: Macmillan, 1963), 47.

Chapter 2: "I'm Sorry": Expressing Regret
1. Robert Fulghum, *All I Really Need to Know I Learned in Kindergarten* (New York: Ballantine, 1986), 4.

Chapter 3: "I Was Wrong": Accepting Responsibility
1. As quoted in Ken Blanchard and Margret McBride, *The One Minute Apology* (New York: Harper Collins, 2003), 1.
2. Ibid., x.
3. Ephesians 5:25–33.
4. Romans 3:23.
5. 1 John 1:8–10.

Chapter 4: "How Can I Make It Right?": Making Restitution

1. The Associated Press, "Thief Returns Cash from Ohio Kettle with Apology," *San Diego Union-Tribune*, December 6, 2012, https://www.sandiegouniontribune.com/sdut-thief-returns-cash-from-ohio-kettle-with-apology-2012dec06-story.html.
2. Everett L. Worthington Jr., *Forgiving and Reconciling: Bridges to Wholeness and Hope* (Downers Grove, IL: InterVarsity, 2003), 205.
3. For an in-depth look at expressing the five love languages among adults, see my books *The 5 Love Languages* (Chicago: Northfield, 2010) and *The 5 Love Languages for Singles* (Chicago: Northfield, 2009).
4. See Luke 19:1–10.

Chapter 5: "I'll Take Specific Steps to Prevent a Recurrence": Planned Change

1. Peter Meyer and Paul Pronovost, "An Apology to Our Readers," *Cape Cod Times*, December 4, 2012, http://www.capecodonline.com/apps/pbcs.dll/article?AID=/20121204/NEWS/121209902.
2. "How It Works," *Alcoholics Anonymous* (New York: Alcoholics Anonymous World Services, Inc., 1976), 59.

Chapter 6: "Can You Find It in Your Heart . . .": Requesting Forgiveness

1. We conducted a survey of more than 370 adults during 2004–2005 at various marriage seminars, and also collected responses on the website garychapman.org. This was a nonscientific survey but included married and single respondents. Most of the respondents at the seminars were married or engaged couples. The survey/questionnaire included seven questions.
2. Remember, for those with a controlling personality, asking forgiveness is out of their comfort zone emotionally. To successfully learn to speak the apology language of requesting forgiveness or, for that matter, any of the apology languages, an extremely controlling individual will likely require the help of an outside party: God, a counselor, a pastor, or a friend who is willing to be honest with him or her.
3. Joanne Kaufman, "Forgive Me!," *Good Housekeeping*, November 2004, 174.

Chapter 8: What If You Don't Want to Apologize?

1. Romans 12:17–19.

Chapter 9: Learning to Forgive

1. "About Forgiveness," https://web.archive.org/web/20110921010133/http://www.forgiveness-Institute.org/html/.
2. Psalm 103:12.
3. Psalm 103:10.

4. Isaiah 43:25.
5. Isaiah 59:2.
6. Romans 6:23.
7. Ibid.
8. See Acts 2:37–39.
9. 1 John 1:9.
10. See Ephesians 4:32.
11. Matthew 7:12.
12. Luke 17:3–4 NKJV.
13. Matthew 18:15–16 NKJV.
14. Romans 12:19.
15. 1 Peter 2:23.
16. Ibid. Richard Francis Weymouth, *The New Testament in Modern Speech* (London: Clarue and Company, 2001).

Chapter 10: Healing Your Family Relationships
1. See Luke 15:11–16.
2. See Luke 15:17–24.

Chapter 12: Truly Sorry, Truly Forgiven
1. Michael S. Woods, *Healing Words: The Power of Apology in Medicine* (Oak Park, IL: Doctors in Touch, 2004), 19.

THE 5 Apology
LANGUAGES

About the Authors

GARY CHAPMAN, PHD, is the author of the bestselling *The 5 Love Languages®* series, which has sold more than 20 million copies worldwide and has been translated into more than fifty languages. He is co-author of *The 5 Apology Languages*, *The 5 Languages of Appreciation in the Workplace*, and forty-five other books. Dr. Chapman travels the world presenting seminars on marriage, family, and relationships, and his radio programs air on more than four hundred stations. For more information, go to www.5lovelanguages.com.

JENNIFER THOMAS, PHD, is a clinical and community psychologist, author, TEDx speaker, and master facilitator for The 5 Love Languages. She is co-author of *The 5 Apology Languages*. For more information, go to www.drjenniferthomas.com.

STRENGTHENING
MILLIONS OF RELATIONSHIPS—
ONE LANGUAGE AT A TIME

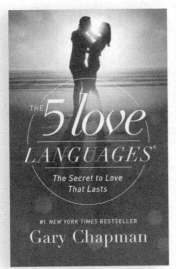

978-0-8024-1270-6

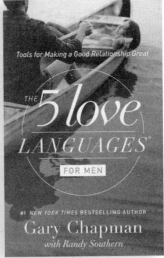

978-0-8024-1272-0

978-0-8024-1284-3

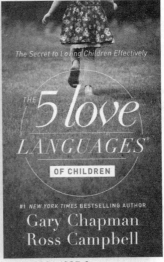

978-0-8024-1285-0

also available as eBooks

When workplace conflict happens,
how do you get back on track?

MAK/NG
TH/NGS
R|GHT
at Work

INCREASE TEAMWORK,
RESOLVE CONFLICT,
AND BUILD TRUST

#1 *New York Times* bestselling author

Gary Chapman,
Jennifer Thomas
& Paul White